AF539856

DESIGN OF SAMPLING PLANS FOR QUALITY CONTROL

DESIGN OF SAMPLING PLANS FOR QUALITY CONTROL

By

Dr. P. Lavanya Kumari

M.Sc, Ph.D., PGDCA, PGDSSA, PGDAS

UGC-Post Doctoral Fellow

Department of Population Studies

Sri Venkateswara University

Tirupati (Andhra Pradesh)

(India)

DISCOVERY PUBLISHING HOUSE PVT. LTD.

NEW DELHI-110 002

Published by:
Tilak Wasan

DISCOVERY PUBLISHING HOUSE PVT. LTD.
4383/4B, Ansari Road, Darya Ganj
New Delhi-110 002 (India)
Phone : +91-11-23279245, 43596064-65
Fax : +91-11-23253475
E-mail : parul.wasan@gmail.com
discoverypublishinghouse@gmail.com
web : www.discoverypublishinggroup.com

***First Edition:* 2012**

ISBN: 978-93-5056-076-1

Design of Sampling Plans for Quality Control

Printed at:
Shree Balaji Art Press
Delhi

Preface

Acceptance sampling is a component of quality control whose objective is to detect quality deficiency with being able to have a counteractive influence. Its philosophy is defensive which means that it however serves for quality control and not for quality improvement.

Sampling plan is a scheme of inspection that specifies not only the number of items to be inspected but also a decision rule to accept or reject the lot. Given a lot of '*N*' items we wish to know *n*, the sample size for inspection and a rule for rejection or acceptance. This requires specification of inspection type, namely *Attribute type* or *Variable type* (by measurements).

The problems studied in this book are motivated by the facilities available in MS-Excel (commonly available software that contains a large number of statistical functions) and an attempt is made to work with designing aspects of Single Sampling Plan (SSP) and Skiplot Sampling Plans (SkSP) using spreadsheet in place of statistical tables as done classically. Similarly the earlier method of working with programs written in FORTRAN or C is now replaced with MS-Excel to evaluate the Operating Characteristic(OC) function of a plan. *Solver,* a powerful optimizing tool available in Excel, is used in this book to derive optimum sampling plans.

The book begins with Chapter 1 which contains introductory concepts and a critical review of literature.

Chapter 2 deals with the determination of the parameters of SSP by modifying the Graf *et al.,* procedure and it is named as MGM. It is a spreadsheet procedure and the solution obtained by MGM is compared with that of conventional algorithm given by Guenther. It is found that the MGM is more economical and it gives better plan quicker than the existing methods.

Chapter 3 covers some computational experiences regarding SkSP in which the reference plan is generated with the help of MGM and the parameters of SkSP are automatically derived on the Excel Sheet. The OC, ASN and the AOQ are obtained with this method and compared with the SkSP plan when the reference plan is based on Guenther[17] and Peach and Littauer[30].

Chapter 4 is concerned with characterization of inspection errors. The theoretical behaviour of type-1 and type-2 risks of misclassification has been modeled by using a truncated Beta distribution. The effect of this distribution on SSP and the resulting SkSP are examined and analyzed. Numerical illustrations highlighting the utility of statistical functions in Excel are exposed in this chapter.

Chapter 5 presents an interesting case of sampling obtained in Oil Company. The problem is that of estimating the oil content in rice bran, which is supplied in bags of fixed size. The quality in each bag is likely to be heterogeneous and the user would take three samples of fixed size, one at the top, middle and bottom of each lot. The sample bran is mixed and the oil content is estimated by a quick chemical procedure. SkSP is applied to this situation in which the user can skip some bags provided that there are '*i*' consecutive bags with expected quality. This would be a mixture of variable type SSP and the usual SkSP. Some statistical results are reported on this issue.

Chapter 6 ends with a conclusion and an outline of the scope for further research.

Dr. P. Lavanya Kumari

Contents

1

Introductory Concepts and Review of Literature

ACCEPTANCE SAMPLING AND RELATED CONCEPTS

Acceptance Sampling is a statistical procedure that specifies a method to accept or reject a lot, basing on the quality observed in the sample drawn from that lot. A sampling plan is a set of rules to execute acceptance sampling, which is known as lot-sentencing procedure. Several basic ideas of acceptance sampling can be found in Mittag & Rinne[28] (1993), Schilling[35] (1989) etc.

According to Dodge[10] (1969), the following are the major types of acceptance sampling.

- Lot by lot sampling by attribute type inspection, in which each unit in the sample is inspected on a go-no-go basis.

- Lot-by-lot sampling by variable type inspection, in which each unit in the sample is measured for a single characteristic, such as weight or strength.
- Continuous sampling of a flow of units by the method of attributes
- Special purpose plans like chain Sampling, Skip-lot Sampling plans etc.

The test-lot from which a sample is drawn should have homogeneous material and should normally represent the true quality derived from the production process. The lot also has to consist of natural units and consequently its size is integer valued like rolls of yarn, electronic devices etc. This assumption excludes bulk goods like wire, paper, sand or fluids, which are not divided into separate sub units.

Acceptance inspection can also be performed in some special cases by 100 per cent testing known as screening. When the quality characteristic to be tested is critical as in the case of shock in an electric iron and the testing is non-destructive then 100 per cent inspection can be adopted and the lot is accepted or rejected basing on the observation. However, screening often leads to unaccountable errors in inspection owing to the fatigue or unstable performance by the inspector. However, screening is not meaningful when the test is either destructive or prohibitively expensive.

The quality observed in the sample usually matches with the quality in the remaining portion of the lot. Mood's[29] theorem given below specifies basic understanding into this aspect.

MOOD'S[29] THEOREM AND ITS IMPORTANCE

Suppose a lot of size *N* has been submitted for inspection. Let the sample size be n and the number of defectives in the sample is *d*. If *d* is large, one can suspect that there will be a large number of defectives in the un-inspected portion of (*N*-*n*) units and the lot should be rejected.

Mood (1943) has attempted this question and proposed a very important theorem that establishes correlation between defectives in the sample and defectives in the remaining lot (not the whole lot).

Let X_N be the number of defective units in the lot under consideration. Define the parameters $\mu_N = E(X_N)$ and $\sigma^2 = V(X_N)$ for whole lot. Now $X_{N-n} = (X_N - X_n)$ denotes the number of defectives in the remainder lot.

Statement

A random sample of size n is taken without replacement from a lot of size N. Define $\mu_N^* = \mu_N\left(1 - \frac{\mu_N}{N}\right)$. *Then the correlation between the number of defective units* X_n *in the sample and the number of defective units* X_{N-n} *in the remainder lot is positive if* $\sigma_N^2 > \mu_N^*$, *zero if* $\sigma_N^2 = \mu_N^*$ *and negative if* $\sigma_N^2 < \mu_N^*$.

The significance of Mood's theorem helps in establishing the nature of relationship between X_n and X_{N-n}.

(*a*) If the correlation is *positive,* it means that X_{N-n} will be small whenever X_n is small. Then lot can be accepted as long as X_n does not exceed a critical number c and this is an adequate strategy [Mittag and Rinne[28](1993)].

(*b*) If the correlation between X_n and X_{N-n} is *negative,* the rule will be reversed. We have to reject the lot, if X_n is small ($\leq c$) and accept otherwise. This is a rule, which is hard to explain to the producer.

(*c*) If X_n and X_{N-n} are *uncorrelated,* it is not possible to use quality in the sample to measure the quality in the lot. A good decision in such cases is either to inspect 100 per ccent or not to inspect the lot at all.

The importance of Mood's theorem lies in the fact that when the product is statistically controlled, a population distribution can be postulated. Most of the acceptance sampling theory assumes that X_n and X_{N-n} are positively correlated. This theorem is very fundamental in the study of sampling plans but not discussed by many standard text books.

TYPES OF SAMPLING PLANS

Depending on whether the test characteristic is discrete or continuous sampling plans can be classified as follows:

- Attributive Sampling Plans or Sampling Plans for Attribute Type Inspection.
- Variable Sampling Plans or Sampling Plans for Variable Type Inspection.

A *defect* is a deviation from the specifications. Any item that does not match with the quality specifications is called *non-conformity* or a *defective* unit. In attributive acceptance sampling, the number of non-conforming units in the sample is counted. In Variable Sampling Plans, a measurement on the quality characteristics becomes the basis for sentencing the lot.

Regardless of whether the sampling is by attributes or variables, a sampling plan specifies the following parameters:

- Size of the sample (n) to be drawn from the lot;
- The statistic to be calculated from the sample data; and
- Exact numerical condition for acceptance or rejection of the lot in the form of a critical number (c).

In addition to the two types, there are other ways of classifying sampling plans.

Plans with Fixed Sample Size

In these plans the sample size is fixed before starting inspection. Some such plans are as follows:

- Single Sampling Plan in which lot sentencing is based only on a single sample from the lot;

- Double Sampling Plan in which a provision is made for examining a second sample whenever the first sample results in a state of indecision;
- Multiple Sampling Plan in which more than two samples are drawn before a decision is taken on the lot.

Plans with Variable Sample Size

Sampling plans of this category are based on Sequential Probability Ratio Test (SPRT) proposed by Wald (1943). One such plan is called Sequential Sampling Plan in which item by item inspection is carried out from the lot, until a decision to accept or reject is arrived at. This plan is suitable for both attribute and variable type inspection.

THE SINGLE SAMPLING PLAN AND ITS RAMIFICATIONS

The design and operation of sampling plan is based on the following concepts:

- **Acceptable Quality Level (AQL):** This is the proportion of defectives (also called fraction defective) with which a lot can be accepted. It is based on the observation that in spite of all the efforts made to avoid defectives, a few occur in the lots and the consumer also agrees to accept such lots. It is usually expressed as a per cent like one per cent or 0.5 per cent defectives being admitted. It is conventionally denoted by p_1.
- **Rejectable Quality Level (RQL) or Lot Tolerance Per cent Defective (LTPD):** This is the worst-case fraction defective at which the consumer is willing to accept the lot. If the observed fraction defective touches RQL, the lot is rejected. It is denoted by p_2 and $p_2 > p_1$. Beyond this level, the lot will be rejected.
- **Producer's Risk:** Since the decision on the lot is based on a random sample, there is every possibility that

one sample may show a higher number defectives than another drawn from the same lot. The producer, after inspection may reject a lot even though the lot really does not warrant rejection! This is called Type-1 error and the probability of committing such an error is known as Producer's risk. This is denoted by α and given by the conditional probability $P(X \leq c \mid p \leq \text{AQL})$, when p is the fraction defective in the sample.

- **Consumer's Risk:** It is the probability of accepting a lot, based on sample, given that the lot truly contains RQL. This error, known as Type-II error occurs because the sample might some times fail to reflect the real quality of the lot. The risk of committing this error is known as Consumer's risk, denoted by β and given by the conditional probability as $P(X \leq c \mid p \geq \text{RQL})$.

For obvious reasons, it is not possible to bring down these two risks to zero but their effect can be accounted for and kept at a minimum, while passing the decision on the lot.

Fixing the value of α at same level, the procedure seeks the best 'acceptance rule' which minimizes β.

Let N, n and c denote respectively the lot size, sample size and the acceptance number. The acceptance number denotes the maximum allowable number of defectives in the sample. The procedure is as follows:

- Select a random sample of n from a lot of size N;
- Inspect all the items included in the sample and let 'd' be the number of defectives in the sample;
- If $d \leq c$, accept the lot after replacing defective pieces found in the sample by non-defective ones;
- If $d > c$, reject the lot or inspect the entire lot and replace all the defective items by the good one's.

THE OPERATING CHARACTERISTIC (OC) FUNCTION

Given a lot of size N with a sample of size n and critical number c, the problem is to evaluate the probability of accepting the lot, denoted by P_a is called the *Operating Characteristic or OC function* of a sampling plan.

The OC function of the plan is specified as $L(p) = P(X \leq c \mid p)$ where X denotes the random variable indicating the count of defective items in the sample. It gives the discriminatory power of the plan to choose between good lots and bad lots. The design of the plan is based on the values of AQL, RQL,α, β, N and p. The OC curve can be found using either Hyper Geometric distribution (type-A) or its approximations like Binomial or Poisson (type-B).

The **type-A OC** function requires the use of Hyper Geometric distribution given by

$$L(p \mid n;c) = \sum_{x=0}^{c} \left[\frac{\binom{M}{x}\binom{N-M}{n-x}}{\binom{N}{n}} \right] \tag{1.1}$$

One has to refer to statistical tables to evaluate (1.1) but it can be easily worked out using Spreadsheet Software like MS-Excel.

The **type-B OC** curve using Binomial distribution is given by

$$L(p \mid n;c) = \sum_{x=0}^{c} \binom{n}{x} p^x (1-p)^{n-x} \tag{1.2}$$

and the OC function using Poisson distribution is given by

$$L(p \mid n;c) = \sum_{x=0}^{c} \left[\frac{(np)^x e^{-np}}{X!} \right] \tag{1.3}$$

These two forms can also be evaluated using Excel functions.

Designing an Admissible Single Sampling Plan (SSP)

A Sampling Plan is said to be *admissible* if it satisfies the conditions

$$L(AQL) \geq 1 - \alpha \tag{1.4a}$$

$$L(RQL) \leq \beta \tag{1.4b}$$

The classical method of designing a SSP is to search for the values of n and c so to satisfy (1.4*a*) and (1.4*b*) as closely as possible. The situation warrants the use of type-B OC curve if $n/N \leq 0.1$ and $p \geq 0.9$. One method is to locate the Poisson parameter $\lambda = np$ corresponding to the two percentiles at (1-α) and β of the Poisson distribution and thereby estimate *n*. The search starts at $c = 0$ and terminates when the ratio $R = np_\beta / np_{1-\alpha}$ crosses the threshold value $R' = RQL/AQL$. This method often gives more than one plan, all of which satisfy one of the two risks exactly but not the other. It is however difficult to get a plan that meets both the risks exactly. This procedure requires cumulative Poisson tables, which are tabulated for specific values of λ and c only.

An interesting problem in the design of the plan is to estimate by an inverse procedure the Poisson parameter $\lambda = np$ such that $P\,(X \leq c \mid np)$ = AQL. The same problem occurs when Binomial distribution is used to define the OC function. In both cases it is difficult to locate the parameter from the cumulative probability distribution.

Let Pos $(c \mid \lambda) = \sum_{i=0}^{c} \frac{\lambda^i}{i!} e^{-\lambda} = \omega$ = be the cumulative Poisson distribution and let

$$Ch[2\lambda \mid 2(c+1)] = \frac{1}{2^{(c+1)}\tau(c+1)} \int_{2\lambda}^{\infty} u^k e^{-u/2} du$$

denote the cumulative Chi-square distribution with parameter 2λ and degrees of freedom $2(c + 1)$.

The relationship between these distributions is given by (see Mittag and Rinne (1993))

$Pos(c \mid \lambda) = 1 - Ch\,[2\lambda \mid 2(c+1)]$

$\Rightarrow Ch\,[2\lambda \mid 2(c+1)] = 1-\omega$

$\Rightarrow \chi^2_{2(c+1);\,1-\omega} = 2\lambda$ from which we get

$$\lambda = 0.5\{\chi^2_{2(c+1);\,1-\omega}\} \tag{1.5}$$

A similar relation between Binomial and F distributions exists given by

$$B(c > n, p) = 1 - F\left[\left(\frac{n-c}{c+1}\right)\left(\frac{p}{1-p}\right) \middle| \, 2(c+1); 2(n-c)\right]$$

where the LHS is the cumulative Binomial distribution up to c denoted by ω and the RHS is the complementary F distribution up to c with $\{2(c+1), 2(n-c)\}$ degrees of freedom. Then the Binomial proportion p can be worked out with the formula for given values of n, c and ω.

$$F_{2(c+1);\,2(n-c);\,1-\omega} = \left(\frac{n-c}{c+1}\right)\left(\frac{p}{1-p}\right) \tag{1.6}$$

Excel has built-in functions BINOMDIST and POISSON to find the OC values and CHINV and FINV to deal with inverse functions. These functions can be used in place of conventional statistical tables to determine n and c. Details of these functions are discussed by Sarma[34] (2001). Consider the following illustration:

Illustration-1.1

Let the plan parameters be $n = 50$, $c = 2$, AQL = 0.05 and RQL = 0.2. Then the Poisson parameter λ at AQL becomes $\lambda_{AQL} = n{*}AQL = 2.5$.

The Excel function POISSON (x, Mean, 1) gives $P(X \le c \mid \lambda) = \sum_{i=0}^{c} \frac{\lambda^i}{i!} e^{-\lambda}$.

The argument '1' indicates cumulative probability and the point probability mass can be obtained by taking this parameter as 0. With these values POISSON(2, 2.5, 1) gives $L(AQL \mid \lambda_{AQL}, c) = 0.5438$. In the same way we get $L(RQL) = 0.0028$ with $c = 2$. In general we can evaluate $L(p \mid \lambda, c)$ for different values of p by taking $\lambda = np$. Thus at AQL, the probability of accepting the lot becomes 0.5438.

Suppose $\alpha = 0.05$ and $\beta = 0.08$ be the advertised risks. In the light of (1.4*a*) and (1.4*b*) this plan is not admissible as it violates (1.4*a*).

In the following illustration we obtain the value of n for a given value of c, α and AQL through appropriate inverse functions.

Illustration 1.2

Suppose $\alpha = 0.05$, AQL = 0.10 and $c = 0$. We can find the Poisson parameter $\lambda = np_{1-\alpha}$ from (1.5) with $1-\omega = 0.95$ in the function CHINV. This gives $\lambda = 2.996$ so that an estimate of n at the AQL would be $n_{AQL} = np_{1-\alpha}/AQL = 29.96 \cong 30$. We can also get another estimate of n at the RQL by this method.

Thus the inverse functions available in Excel serve as quick tools to determine the parameters of a SSP instead of referring to tables, which were designed for fixed range of inputs.

DOUBLE AND MULTIPLE SAMPLING PLANS

Double Sampling Plan (DSP) is a procedure in which a second sample is required under certain circumstances before the lot is sentenced. The DSP contains four parameters:

n_1 = size of the first sample;
c_2 = acceptance number of the first sample;
n_2 = size of the second sample; and
c_2 = acceptance number for both samples.

When the number of defectives in the first sample d_1 is greater than c_1 but less than or equal to c_2, a second sample of size n_2 is taken. If the number of defectives in combined sample $(d_1 + d_2)$ e" c_2 the lot is rejected. The probability of acceptance becomes

$P_a = p_a^1 + p_a^2$, where p_a^1, p_a^2 are the acceptance probabilities of first and second samples.

An interesting aspect of DSP is that the inspector gets a second chance before sentencing lot in case of ambiguity. The question is on what do with the second sample, when the critical number is reached. One may opt for a complete inspection of n_2 items or curtail the inspection.

The Average Sample Number is a measure of effort required in judging the lots. It is given by ASN = $n_1 + n_2 (1-p_1)$ where p_1 is the probability of lot dispositioning decision on the first sample.

Double Sampling can be designed in such a way that it get the same accuracy as if a single sampling plan of size $n_1 + n_2$ was adopted. The convenience lies in disposing the lots in the first sample itself when the quality is good (or bad). Double Sampling Plans with minimum ATI have been derived by Craig[7] (1981).

The Multiple Sampling Plan (MSP) is an extension of DSP where the inspector takes several changes before disposing the lot. Though MSP has the advantage in recommending smaller samples at each stage it is a complex procedure to implement.

CONTINUOUS SAMPLING PLANS

In some cases production is done in such a way that lots are not formed at the time of inspection. Items that come out of a conveyor belt of a production-line or yarn coming out of a spinning section are some examples. Since there is no lot, the question of accepting the lot does not arise. However, inspection is carried according to a procedure from the production line itself and the quality is assessed. Dodge[8] (1943) has proposed such a plan and called it Continuous Sampling Plan (CSP). By its very nature, the CSP is not a sentencing procedure but acts as an audit that ensures the quality of the items, which leave the production line. It is a properly defined mixture of screening and sampling.

Dodge[8] (1943), has proposed the CSP-1, which is a mixture of screening and sampling. At the start of the plan all units are inspected 100 per cent. If '*i*' consecutive non-defectives are found, screening is stopped and a fraction '*f*' is inspected. If $f = 1/10$, it means one unit is selected at random out of 10 in the order and it is inspected. If the sampled unit is non-defective, we continue sampling from the next 10 units. If it is defective, we stop sampling and we resort to screening.

The objective of designing CSP-1 is to ensure that the outgoing fraction defective, average outgoing quality limit (AOQL) is kept at a minimum. The parameters (i, f) of the plan can be determined corresponding to an AOQL value.

There are many variations of CSP-1 resulting in CSP-2 and CSP-3. Wald and Wolfowitz (1945) have proposed another CSP type plan.

A Graphical Method of selecting the parameters for CSP-1, CSP-2, and CSP-R under a Non-replacement Assumption was developed by Abraham[1] (1971), which is like a nomogram.

ALGORITHMS FOR DESIGNING A SINGLE SAMPLING PLAN

The conventional approach to design a sampling plan is based on the OC curve such that the plan has admissible risks at AQL and RQL. Theoretically there exists several admissible plans for a given set of input parameters and we have to choose the one that minimizes the sample size n. Analytical procedures leading to a closed form solution are not possible in case of Hypergeometric, Binomial or Poisson distributions and we have to use search methods. The Guenther's[17] search algorithm (1959) and the Peach-Littaur's algorithm[30] (1946) are two important search procedures that are popularly used.

Hailey[20] (1980) has given a computerized approach for determining a SSP that yields the minimum sample size. The other methods include the procedure by Graf *et al.* (1987) and the Phillips system. Mittag and Rinne[28] (1993) have discussed these algorithms in detail. Chakraborthy[5] (1989) has formulated the single sampling plan problem as a non-linear mixed integer goal-programming problem.

In the following section we review and compare these methods:

(*a*) Guenther's[17] Search Algorithm

This algorithm starts with $c = 0$ and $n = 1$. With the underlying distribution like Hyper Geometric, Binomial or Poisson, the OC value $L(\text{RQL})$ is evaluated at the RQL. In the outer loop by taking $c = 0$ we increase n stepwise by one, until $L(\text{RQL}) \leq \beta$. Using these n and c if $L(\text{AQL}) \geq (1-\alpha)$ is satisfied, we have found the plan with minimal sample size. Otherwise take $c = c+1$ in the outer loop and repeat the inner loop with $n = c$. The entire procedure should be repeated until the admissibility conditions are satisfied. The plan derived by this method will have the property that among all admissible plans it has the minimum difference between effective and specified producer's risk and maximum difference between effective and specified consumer's risk. This algorithm can be implemented in any programming language or even in the Excel spreadsheet with Solver module.

(*b*) Peach-Littauer's[30] Search Algorithm

This is another procedure proposed by Peach and Littauer (1946) to determine n and c, when the underlying distribution is Poisson. Given the values of AQL, RQL, α and β this method initially starts with $c = 0$. The OC percentiles using Chi Square approximation, given by $q_1(c) = \dfrac{\chi^2_{2(c+1);\,1-\beta}}{2.RQL}$ and $q_2(c) =$

$\frac{\chi^2_{2(c+1);\,1-\beta}}{2.\,RQL}$ and $q_2(c) = \frac{\chi^2_{2(c+1);\,\alpha}}{2.\,AQL}$ are calculated iteratively for different values of $c = 0, 1, 2, 3\ldots$, until $q_1(c) \le q_2(c)$. The value of n corresponding to this c is the smallest integer, which lies between $q_1(c)$ and $q_2(c)$.

(c) Graf, Henning, Stange, Wilrich algorithm (Graf *et al*[14] algorithm)

This is a one step formula to determine n and c, which is an alternative to Guenther's search algorithm when the statistic follows Binomial distribution. The approximation formula proposed by Graf *et al* is

$$n \cong \frac{1}{4}\left(\frac{Z_{1-\alpha} + Z_{1-\beta}}{\varphi_2 - \varphi_1}\right)^2 - \frac{1}{4\varphi_1\varphi_2} \tag{1.7}$$

where ϕ_1 = Arc sin $\varepsilon\left(P^p_{0.5}\right) \approx -\sqrt{\frac{2}{\pi}(c+0.73)}$ where $P^p_{0.5} \approx \frac{c+\frac{2}{3}}{n}$.,

ϕ_2 = Arc sin $\left(\sqrt{RQL}\right)$ and Z_ω is defined to be the percentile of order ω from $N(0, 1)$. With this n, one obtains the acceptance number c as

$$c \cong n.\,\{\sin^2\varphi^*\} - 0.5 \tag{1.8}$$

where $\phi^* := \frac{1}{2}(\phi_1 + \phi_2)\left(1 - \frac{1}{8n\varphi_1\varphi_2}\right) + \left[\frac{Z_{1-\alpha} + Z_{1-\beta}}{4\sqrt{n}}\right]$

This formula is easy to implement but the admissibility conditions are not always satisfied by the plan. In chapter-2 we modify this plan by attaching a search procedure around the solution space.

(*d*) Philips System

This is also an approximation procedure proposed by the Dutch electro corporation Philips to construct sampling plans $(N\,;\,n\,;\,c)$ with given lot size N. This formula is based on the elasticity of the OC function at the indifference quality level

(IQL). When the test statistic follows Poisson distribution the following approximation formulae for determining n and c are used by the Philips system.

$$c \approx \frac{\pi}{2}\left[\varepsilon\left(P_{0.5}^{p}\right)\right]^{2} - 0.73 \text{ and } n \approx \frac{c+\frac{2}{3}}{P\frac{p}{0.5}}, \tag{1.9}$$

$$\text{where } \varepsilon\left(P_{0.5}^{p}\right) = -2\left[\frac{\left(nP_{0.5}^{p}\right)^{c+1}}{c!}\right]c^{-n}P_{0.5}^{p}$$

or

$$\varepsilon\left(P_{0.5}^{p}\right) \approx -\sqrt{\frac{2}{\pi}(c+0.73)} \text{ where } P_{0.5}^{p} \approx \frac{c+\frac{2}{3}}{n}. \tag{1.10}$$

Other methods include mathematical programming like the one given by Chakraborthy[5] (1989).

In the following section we discuss a spreadsheet solution to derive the plan using the method given by Graf *et al.*:

COMPUTER PROGRAMS FOR SAMPLING PLANS

As an alternative to reference to sampling plan tables, efforts were made by researchers to develop a computer program that gives the optimum sampling plan for the given inputs.

Snyder and Storer[36] (1972) have prepared a FORTRAN program to determine Single Sampling Plans with given AQL, RQL, α and β. Their approach is based on Poisson distribution and the program gives four different plans. Plan-1 gives minimum value of n and will be close to β risk. Plan-2 give maximum n and will be close to α risk. The next two samples will have sample sizes, which will minimize the weighted sum and ratio of two risks respectively.

Hailey[20] (1980) developed a FORTRAN program to determine the minimum size sampling plan using Guenther's search procedure. This program is based on Binomial and Poisson OC functions and yields an admissible plan. Separate subroutines for Binomial and Poisson have been used for this purpose.

Spreadsheet programs are convenient to deal with statistical functions and hence sampling plans can also be studied in on spreadsheets instead of writing programs. Further graphs relating to the sampling plans can be directly prepared and simulated on spreadsheet.

SKIP LOT SAMPLING PLAN

Dodge[10] (1955) has originally developed the Skip Lot Sampling Plan (SkSP) as an extension of the Continuous Sampling Plan (CSP) for lots, which he called SkSP-1. Under this method each lot or unit of production is inspected by a single determination (called screening). When i consecutive lots are found free of defects, the method of inspection is relaxed and a fraction f of the incoming lots is only inspected (called sampling). The idea is to reduce the effort of inspection when the quality history is found to be good in a series of lots. Interestingly in this method, certain percent of defective lots are likely to escape inspection and reach the customer. One measure of performance of this plan is the percentage of lots accepted by the procedure, denoted by $L_{Sk}(p)$ where p is the probability of accepting a lot by the sampling procedure.

In SkSP-2 the decision to accept or reject a lot depends on the outcome of a reference plan, which is usually taken as Single Sampling Plan (SSP). The inspection procedure is similar to that of SkSP-1 except that lot sentencing is based on the outcome of the reference plan. The following are the steps to implement SkSP-2:

(*a*) Start inspection with *screening* in which *each* incoming lot is inspected by SSP until 'i' successive lots are accepted ($i \geq 2$).

(*b*) Switch to *skip mode* in which only one out of 'k' lots is randomly selected and inspected. If this lot is accepted, the remaining (k-1) lots are also accepted and out of the next k lots, another one is selected and inspected. This method is continued until the single lot under skipping inspection is rejected, in which case we switch back to screening.

It is assumed that every rejected lot is replaced with a good one. Perry[31] (1973) and Dodge and Perry[10] (1971) have given a basic treatment of SkSP by using Markov Chain approach to determine the percentage of lots accepted under the plan. Soundararajan and Vijayaraghavan[38] (1989) have proposed a modification, called SkSP-3 in which the idea is to inspect next k consecutive lots whenever a lot under skipping inspection is rejected (instead of immediately switching to screening). If any of these lots is rejected then screening inspection is repeated.

Here are some basic results of interest:

1. The proportion of lots accepted by the plan is given by

$$L_{sk}(p) = \frac{(1-f)L(p)^i + fL(p)}{(1-f)L(p)^i + f}$$

where p = incoming quality level

$L(p)$ = acceptance probability based on the reference plan

f = sampling fraction

This function is considered as the OC function of SkSP-2.

2. The Average Fraction Inspected is given by

$$AFI_{sk} = \frac{f}{(1-f)L(p)^i + f}$$

3. If the reference plan is a single sampling plan with sample size *n*, then the Average Sample Number of the SkSP-2 is $ASN_{sk}(P) = n.AFI_{sk}(P)$.
4. The Average Outgoing Quality (AOQ) is the proportion of the outgoing non-conforming lots.

It is clear that given the values of *i* and *f*, the performance of SkSP depends on the characteristics of the reference plan and the incoming lot quality.

Not many research articles are reported in literature on SkSP in the recent years. However many interesting modifications have been made in the study of Continuous Sampling Plans which can be directly extended to SkSP procedures.

There are two important aspects of working with these plans. The first one is related to the development of a theoretical basis for the inspection procedure and the other one is the numerical evaluation of the plan.

In chapter-3 these aspects are discussed.

INSPECTION ERRORS AND THEIR INFLUENCE ON SAMPLING PLANS

One of the basic assumptions in the attribute type inspection is that the inspection process is free of errors. In practice it is not so and errors occur in inspection. This leads to misclassification of good items into bad and vice versa.

(*a*) Problem of Misclassification

An attribute gage is used to compare a dimension with standards and the inspector classifies the item into good or bad basing on the result of gage test. Over a period of time the gage itself becomes faulty, leading to wrong acceptance or rejection. It is also possible that the operators may not perform consistently even though they use the same gage. The concept of *measurement system analysis* focuses on two aspects of errors of a measurement system namely: (*a*) Repeatability; and (*b*) Reproducibility.

- **Repeatability:** It is the variation in the measurements obtained by one measuring instrument when used several times by one appraiser while measuring the identical characteristic on the same part.
- **Reproducibility:** It is the variation in average of measurements made by different appraisers using the same measuring instrument when measuring the identical characteristic on the same part.

The gage is acceptable, if all the measurement decisions agree. In the above case, each part is measured four times. If the measurements do not agree the gage should be improved or reevaluated.

(*b*) Probabilistic aspects of Inspection Errors

There are two types of inspection errors similar to those, committed in tests of hypothesis. These are as follows:

Type I Inspection error: It is the error of classifying a good item as bad item.

Type II Inspection error: It is the error of classifying a bad item as good item.

Mittag and Rinne[28] (1993) used the following notation to explain inspection errors.

Define $T = 0$ if sample unit is 'good'

$= 1$ if sample unit is 'bad'

T is unobservable stochastic variable that represents the true state of the unit.

Define $K = 0$ if sample unit is classified as 'good'

$= 1$ if sample unit is classified as 'bad'

K represents the outcome of inspection of a sample unit. The risks associated with type I and type II errors are basically conditional probabilities defined as follows:

Type I risk: (ε)

$\varepsilon = P\ (K = 1 \mid T = 0) = P$ (classifying a good item as bad)

$$= \frac{P(K=1, T=0)}{P(T=0)}$$

Type II risk: (ϕ)

$\phi = P\ (K = 0 \mid T = 1) = P$ (Classifying a bad item as good)

$$= \frac{P(K=0, T=1)}{P(T=1)}$$

It is practically difficult to estimate these risks exactly. Bauer (1987) has observed that they can take values as high as $\varepsilon = 0.4$ and $\phi = 0.9$.

(c) Apparent Fraction Defective

Let the inspection process be carried out with one inspector using go-no-go gage and let p be the true fraction defective of the incoming lots. Since p is usually not known we can investigate the expected value or the observed fraction defective for a lot, in case of 100 per cent inspection. The probability that a defective unit is correctly classified as defective becomes $P\ (K=1 \mid T=1) = 1 - \phi$.

Since $0 \le \phi \le 1$, only when type-I error is present the true fraction defective is under-estimated as $p+(1-p)\phi$. Again when type II error is present certain defective will be classified as good. Since $0 \le \varepsilon \le 1$ and $(1-p)$ is the proportion of good items and it is over-estimated as $p(1-\phi)$.

The inspector may commit one of these two errors but only one error at a time. The two events will be mutually exclusive and the expected fraction defective becomes

$$\pi = p(1-\phi) + (1-p)\,\varepsilon \tag{1.11}$$

This is called the observed fraction defective or *apparent fraction defective.*

It is also possible that an inspector may consistently commit only type I error or type II error over a period of time. It is a chronic bias. Thus when inspection errors are present, the true fraction defective of a lot will distorted. It will show its effect on the performance measure of the sampling plan, namely the OC function.

(*d*) Behaviour of OC Function in Presence of Errors

Consider the case of a single sampling plan with parameters n and c. Assume that a type B OC function is used with Binomial distribution. When the lot fraction defective is π, the OC function in presence of errors becomes

$$L_e(p,n,c) = \sum_{i=0}^{c} \binom{n}{i} \pi^i (1-\pi)^{n-i}$$

$$= \sum_{i=0}^{c} \binom{n}{i} \left[(p(1-\varphi)+(1-p)\varepsilon\right]^i \left[p\varphi+(1-p)(1-\varepsilon)\right]^{n-i} \quad (1.12)$$

Since, the lot sentencing (decision making) is based on apparent fraction defective π instead of p, the ability of the plan to distinguish between good and bad lots depends on the empirical OC function given in (1.12). In fact, the results of the plan do not match with the specifications for which the plan was originally constructed.

When only type I error occurs we get $\phi = 0$ and $\varepsilon > 0$. Then $\pi = p + (1\text{-p})\varepsilon$, which is an under estimate of p. This leads to $\varepsilon > p$ and results in a decrease in the acceptance probability of the lot.

It means

$L_e(p, n, c) < L(p)$, for $p \, \varepsilon \, [0,1]$

When only type II error is present, we get $\pi = p\,(1\text{-}\,\phi)$, which is less than p. This leads to

$L_e(p, n, c) > L(p)$, for $p \, \varepsilon \, [0,1]$

More details on these effects can be found in Mittag and Rinne[28] (1993).

(*e*) ATI, AOQ and Other Measures

With reference to the single sampling plan under rectifying inspection it is known that

$$ATI(p) = \frac{n + (N-n)\left[1 - L(p)\right]}{1-p} \tag{1.13}$$

In the presence of inspection errors, the empirical ATI function becomes

$$ATI_c(p) = \frac{n + (N-n)\left[1 - L_e(p)\right]}{p\varphi + (1-p)(1-\varepsilon)} \tag{1.14}$$

The Average outgoing quality is also affected by the apparent fraction defective and given by

$$AOQ_e = \left\{\frac{p}{N}\right\} \frac{n\varphi + (N-n)\left[p\varphi + (1-p)(1-\varepsilon)L_3(p) + \varphi\{1 - L_e(p)\}\right]}{p\varphi + (1-p)(1-\varepsilon)}$$

The effect of these errors on the AOQ function has been discussed by Mittag and Rinne(1993). It is observed that the effect of errors on the AOQ is similar to the effect on the OC curve.

In chapter-4 a theoretical model to estimate the apparent fraction defective using truncated Beta distribution is developed.

REVIEW OF RECENT LITERATURE

The new results and procedures proposed in this thesis are derived from fundamental concepts of sampling inspection. There are very few papers for which the results of this thesis can be viewed as extensions. However some interesting aspects discussed by various researchers are reviewed here.

Brush and Bernard[4] (1990) have developed a procedure to estimate the out going quality in the context of quality assurance program. They have proposed an estimator called QMP (Quality Measurement Plan) estimator. It is claimed to be robust and provides an interval estimate for quality.

Chun and Rinks[6] (1998) have proposed three types of producer's and consumer's risks and called them classical, modified and Bayes risks. This classification is related to inspection errors. They have demonstrated these results using Binomial-Beta combination for Bayes estimators.

A comprehensive survey of literature on inspection errors is given by Dorris and Foote (1978).

Greenberg and Stokes[15] (1992) have studied the problem of estimating non-conformance rates using zero defect sampling with rectification. They have proposed a non-parametric estimator which is very much similar to Horvitz-Thompson estimator (Cochran(1977)).

Greengerg and Stokes[16] (1995) have studied the effect of inspection errors on repetitive testing which is a common procedure when rejections are costly. They have constructed a model from which they expected benefit of n retests could be calculated and maximized. This study has specific application to semiconductor devices.

Sufficient focus was given on estimating the non-conformity rate in zero-defect sampling by Hahn[19] (1986). Zaslavsky[42] (1988) has extended the estimation procedure to *c*-defect sampling and derived confidence intervals. The objective is to estimate the total number of defective units in accepted lots.

A different type of inspection plan based on Maximum Allowable Per cent Defective (MAPD) has been developed by Soundararajan[37] (1975) which was further explored by Suresh & Ram Kumar (1996) and Suresh, Radhakrishnan and Alamedu[39] (2002). These plans are of the type CSP-1 ($c = 2$) and the idea of Maximum Allowable AOQ has been used to derive matching sampling plans. Suresh, Radhakrishnan and Kavitha[40] (2002) have used the idea MAAOQ to derive a

TNT – Plan and constructed tables. These plans are matched with plans indexed through MAPD and AOQL.

Beainy and Case[3] (1981) have developed performance measures of the AOQ and ATI type when inspection is imperfect. Using the idea of signal detection theory, they have demonstrated that these measures are influenced by the magnitude of inspection errors.

Johnson, Kotz and Rodriguez[22] (1986) gave a detailed narration on the effects of imperfect inspection on Double Sampling and link sampling. Harichandra and Srivenkataramana[21] (1982) have developed theory on link sampling for attributes.

In the recent years user-friendly software has been developed to work with sampling plans for instance *statgraphics, QM for windows, Indostat* etc have specific modules to deal with sampling plans.

Ghosh (1988,1989,1990)[11,12,13] has developed optimum continuous sampling plans under different condition.

Chakraborthy and Umesh Kumar[5] (1989) have used GERT (Graphic Evaluation and Review Technique) approach to analyze inspection errors, which is a non-conventional approach.

Martz and Zimmer[27] (1990) have used non-parametric approach to estimate the per cent defectives in accepted lots. Their approach is called Bayes-Empirical-Bayes (BEB) approach.

FOCUS OF THE BOOK

The focus of the book is on two aspects:

(1) Computational aspects in determining the parameters of a plan. The use of spreadsheet solutions in place of reference to tables is highlighted.

(2) Misclassification and inspection errors, their characterization, computational facilities and their impact on the sampling plan.

2

A Spreadsheet Solution to Design Single Sampling Plan for Attribute Inspection

SPREADSHEET SOLUTION TO GRAF *ET AL*'S[14] METHOD

Derivation of a Single Sampling Plan (SSP) by running C or FORTRAN programs can be replaced with spreadsheet solutions. In this chapter the Graf *et al* procedure is implemented on the Excel spreadsheet leading to a new method called Modified Graf *et al* Method (MGM). Two other methods viz., Peach-Littauer's method and the ATI based method are also implemented on spreadsheet. The built-in functions for ArcSin and Standard Normal distributions can be utilized to evaluate the expressions in the Graf *et al* procedure discussed in chapter-1.

This one step formula to determine n and c, is based on Binomial distribution type OC function. The approximation formula proposed by Graf *et al* given in (1.7) requires the evaluation of the following terms

- $\phi_1 = \text{Arc sin}\left(\sqrt{AQL}\right)$
- $\phi_2 = \text{Arc sin}\left(\sqrt{RQL}\right)$
- Z_ω = percentile of order ω from $N(0,1)$
- $\phi^* := \frac{1}{2}(\phi_1 + \phi_2)\left(1 - \frac{1}{8n\varphi_1\varphi_2}\right) + \left[\frac{Z_{1-\alpha} + Z_{1-\beta}}{4\sqrt{n}}\right]$ (2.1)
- $n \cong \frac{1}{4}\left(\frac{Z_{1-\alpha} + Z_{1-\beta}}{\varphi_2 - \varphi_1}\right)^2 - \frac{1}{4\varphi_1\varphi_2}$ sample size) (2.2)
- $c \cong n.\{\sin^2\varphi^*\}-0.5$ (acceptance number)

The Excel template to work with these formulae is shown in figure-2.1.

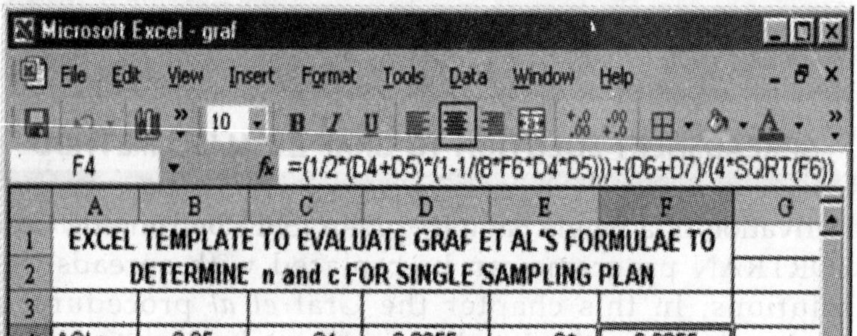

Microsoft Excel - graf

File Edit View Insert Format Tools Data Window Help

F4 =(1/2*(D4+D5)*(1-1/(8*F6*D4*D5)))+(D6+D7)/(4*SQRT(F6))

	A	B	C	D	E	F	G
1	EXCEL TEMPLATE TO EVALUATE GRAF ET AL'S FORMULAE TO						
2	DETERMINE n and c FOR SINGLE SAMPLING PLAN						
3							
4	AQL=	0.05	Q1=	0.2255	Q*=	0.3655	
5	RQL=	0.13	Q2=	0.3689	1-COSQ^2	0.1278	
6	ALFA=	0.05	Z(1-alfa)=	1.6449	n =	111	
7	BETA =	0.08	Z(1-beta)=	1.4051	c =	14	
8							
9							

GRAF

Ready NUM

Fig. 2.1: Excel template for Graf *et al*'s procedure

This template gives a plan with n = 111 and c = 14 for the given input values. The plan is however not admissible as it gives a higher β-risk (0.522) than the specified value (0.08).

In the following section a new plan is derived with the same n and values of c modified in such a way that the plan has risks *closer to the specifications.*

MODIFIED GRAF *ET AL* METHOD (MGM)

Let the values given by Graf *et al* method be n_0 and c_0, which may not always yield an admissible plan. The admissibility of the plan can be verified by evaluating the achieved risks at AQL and RQL. The difference between the target risk and achieved risk is a measure of the deviation from the admissible plan. By searching in the neighborhood of n_0 and c_0, it is possible to locate a plan with admissible risks, by using spreadsheet functions. By fixing the value of n as n_0 we can change the value of c_0 until the admissibility conditions are satisfied as closely as possible. This search usually requires a few trails and can be automatized by using *solver* in Excel. Consider the following proposition.

Proposition 2.1: A measure of performance of the plan is the Root Squared Deviation (RSD) defined in terms of Holder's norm $Lp = || \Sigma(g_i - G_i)^p ||^{1/p}$, where g_i and G_i are the Expected and Observed values at i^{th} data point. Taking p = 2 we get

$$RSD = || [(1-\alpha)-L_{AQL}(n_o, c_o)]^2 + [\beta-L_{RQL}(n_o, c_o)]^2 ||^{1/2} \quad (2.3)$$

Proposition 2.2: RSD is convex in c and hence a unique minimum exists at $c = c_{opt}$.

Proof: By definition Total Squared Deviation is given by (TSD) = $[(1-\alpha)-L_{AQL}(n_o, c_o)]^2 + [\beta-L_{RQL}(n_o, c_o)]^2$ which is the sum of squared errors at AQL and RQL respectively. The first component is a decreasing function of c and the second one is an increasing function and their sum is convex in c. The RSD being a real valued function of TSD is also convex.

Hence the proof.

The formulae given by Graf *et al* can be modified as follows.

Step 1: Compute the values of n and c using (2.1) & (2.2) of chapter-1 and call them n_0 and c_0 respectively.

Step 2: Calculate L(AQL) and L(RQL) for this plan.

Step 3: If the admissibility conditions are satisfied, it is the optimum plan; else go to next step.

Step 4: Fixing the value of n at n_0 decrease the value of c from c_0 to c_0-1 and evaluate RSD using (2.3).

Step 5: Repeat the procedure until RSD reaches minimum for some value of $c = c_{opt}$.

Step 6: The plan (n, c) with $n = n_0$ and $c = c_{opt}$ is the required plan by the Modified Graf's Method (MGM).

The following is the stepwise procedure for implementing MGM on the spreadsheet.

IMPLEMENTING MGM ON SPREADSHEET

MGM is implemented in two stages. Stage-1 deals with derivation of n_0 and c_0 from Graf *et al* procedure. Stage-2 uses solver tool to reach optimum c iteratively.

Stage-1: Implementing Graf *et al*'s Procedure

Step 1: Input the values of AQL, RQL, α and β in specific cells of the sheet.

Step 2: Enter the formulae in various cells as shown on next page. Labels for the variables may be given on the left of formulae cells.

Step 3: This completes the determination of n and c as n_0 and c_0.

Step 4: By changing the input values, the output gets automatically updated.

CELL	Expression
D2	= ASIN (SQRT (B2))
D3	= ASIN (SQRT (B3)
F2	= (1/2*(D2+D3)*(1-1/(8*H4*D2*D3))) + (D4+D5)/ (4*SQRT(H4))
F3	= 1-(COS (F2)^2
D4	= NORMSINV (1-B4)
D5	= NORMSINV (1-B5)
F4	= (1/4*((D4+D5)/(D3-D2))^2) - 1/(4*D2*D3)
F5	= (H4*F3)-0.5
H4	= CEILING (F4,1)
H5	= ROUND (F5,0)

Stage-2 : Search for near optimum _n_ and _c_ by using Solver

The following are the steps of the optimization procedure. Iterations are performed with $c_1 = c_0$ and $c_{i+1} = c_i$-1 until the RSD(c_i) ≤ RSD(c_{i+1}). The Solver module in Excel uses this condition to terminate the search.

Step-5: Enter the formulae as shown below.

Cell	Formula	Result at the ith iteration
A10	= A9+1	
B9	= BINOMDIST (A9,H4, B2,1)	L_{AQL} ($n_{o,}$ c_i) = OC at AQL with $n_{o,}$ c_i
C9	= BINOMDIST(A9,H4, B3,1)	L_{RQL} (n_o , c_i) = OC at RQL with $n_{o,}$ c_i
D9	= SQRT(((1-B4)-B9)^ 2+(B5-C9)^2)	RSD_i = SQRT([(1-α)-L_{AQL}(n_o , c_i)]^2 + [β-L_{RQL}(n_o , c_i]^2)
B10	= BINOMDIST(A10,H4, B2,1)	L_{AQL} (n_o , c_{i+1})
C10	= BINOMDIST(A10,H4, B3,1)	L_{RQL} (n_o , c_{i+1})
D10	= SQRT(((1-B4)-B10)^ 2+(B5-C10)^2)	RSD_{i+1} = SQRT ([(1-α)- L_{AQL}(n_o , c_{i+1})]^2 + [β- L_{RQL} (n_o , $c_{i+1)}$]^2)

Step-6: Copy the c value from H5 to A9.

Step-7: Put cursor on cell A9 (Destination cell).

Step-8: Select Solver from Tools option and fill in the details of the wizard, with target cell A9 and changing cell also as A9.

Step-9: Indicate the constraint as D9 < D10 so that the iterations are run until the difference (D9–D10) becomes negative. Once this condition is reached, *Solver* automatically stops iterations and the final values at A9 will be c_{opt}.

The complete procedure can be saved as a template so that simulation can be performed to assess the sensitivity of the procedure. The Excel template for obtaining the near optimum plan is given in figure-2.2.

Microsoft Excel - Mgm

D3 =ASIN(SQRT(B3))

	A	B	C	D	E	F	G
1	EXCEL TEMPLATE TO EVALUATE GRAF'S FORMULA FOR n and c						
2	AQL=	0.0787	Q1=	0.2844	Q*=	0.4008	
3	RQL=	0.1536	Q2=	0.4027	1-COSQ^2	0.1522	
4	ALFA=	0.05	Z(1-alfa)=	1.6449	n =	164	
5	BETA =	0.08	Z(1-beta)=	1.4051	c =	24	
6							
7	SOLVER USING HOLDER'S NORM				MGM Plan		
8	i = AdjC	D1i=1-AL1	D2i=B1	RSDi	n =	164	
9	18	0.942	0.069	0.0137	c =	18	
10	19	0.966	0.106	0.0305			
11							
12	STEPS:						
13	1.CHANGE INPUT VALUES LIKE AQL,RQL,ALFA AND BETA IF YOU WANT						
14	2.COPY THE VALUE OF H5 IN THE CELL A9						
15	3.PUT CURSOR ON THE CELL A						
16	4. TOOLS>SOLVER>SOLVE						

MGM | Ready | CAPS NUM

Fig. 2.2: Excel Template for implementing MGM

COMPUTATIONAL EXPERIENCE AND SENSITIVITY

The MGM, which can be easily implemented on the Excel sheet without reference to tables and program codes, has been experimented over a wide range of input parameters and the optimal solution for each case has been obtained. The behaviour of RSD is also verified and the findings are reported in table-2.1(a),(b) and (c) (*See on pages 32, 33 and 34*).

Illustration 2.1

Let AQL = 0.05 and α = 0.05. For different values of β and RQL the behavior of RSD with respect to c is shown in tables-2.1(a)-(c). It can be observed that the plan given by MGM attains both admissibility and minimum RSD.

Hence near optimum plans shown in bold face in the tables-2.1(*a*)-(*c*) can be developed with the help of the Spreadsheet Template. The near optimum solution satisfies the advertised risks quiet closely. The behaviour of RSD is shown in figure-2.3 (*See on page 35*). The RSD can be interpreted as the total percentage error (deviation) in the plan when compared to the specified risks.

- We note that in plan-1 there was about 44.5 per cent error with the original *n* and *c*, which was brought down to 0.4 per cent by decreasing *c* from 14 to 9.
- In plan-4 when β is increased to 0.10 the percentage error has decreased from 44.5 per cent to 3.3 per cent and *c* has decreased from 13 to 8.
- Again in plan-7 with β as 0.12, the optimal *c* has decreased from 11 to 8 with percentage error decreasing from 31 per cent to 0.5 per cent.
- On an average with the chosen parameter the search was terminated in a maximum of 5 iterations.

- It is also observed that higher the gap between AQL and RQL, smaller will be the number of iterations required to find c_{opt}.

Table 2.1(a): Sensitivity of the plan with β = 0.08

Values of RSD with AQL = 0.05, α = 0.05 and β = 0.08			
c	RQL=0.13 n = 111 C = 14	RQL=0.15 n = 76 c = 11	RQL=0.17 n = 56 c = 9
	Plan-1	**Plan-2**	**Plan-3**
14	0.4446		
13	0.3329		
12	0.2265		
11	0.1334	0.4506	
10	0.0578	0.3236	
9	**0.0044**	0.2041	0.4358
8	0.0678	0.1034	0.2957
7	0.1548	**0.0245**	0.1681
6	0.2795	0.0467	0.0659
5	0.4389	0.1425	**0.0152**
4	0.6115	0.2903	0.1103
3	0.7653	0.4870	0.2664
2	0.8737	0.6931	0.4916
1	0.9304	0.8524	0.7311
0	0.9500	0.9332	0.8970
Near Optimum Plan	**(111,9)**	**(76,7)**	**(56,5)**

(Figures in bold face indicate the minimum RSD)

Table 2.1(b): Sensitivity of the plan with $\beta = 0.10$

Values of RSD with AQL = 0.05, $\alpha = 0.05$ and $\beta = 0.10$			
c	RQL = 0.13 n = 102 C = 13	RQL = 0.15 n = 70 c = 10	RQL = 0.17 n = 52 c = 8
	Plan-4	**Plan-5**	**Plan-6**
14			
13	0.4454		
12	0.3288		
11	0.2166		
10	0.1177	0.4187	
9	0.0365	0.2865	
8	**0.0326**	0.1643	0.3696
7	0.1087	0.0630	0.2266
6	0.2160	**0.0192**	0.1029
5	0.3643	0.1068	**0.0065**
4	0.5407	0.2379	0.0867
3	0.7130	0.4270	0.2278
2	0.8457	0.6439	0.4459
1	0.9214	0.8268	0.6976
0	0.9499	0.9278	0.8862
Near Optimum Plan	**(102,8)**	**(70,6)**	**(52,5)**

(Figures in bold face indicate the minimum RSD)

Table 2.1(c): Sensitivity of the plan with $\beta = 0.12$

Values of RSD with AQL = 0.05, α = 0.05 and β = 0.12			
c	RQL=0.13 n = 94 c = 11	RQL=0.15 n = 65 c = 10	RQL=0.17 n = 48 c = 7
	Plan-7	**Plan-8**	**Plan-9**
14			
13			
12			
11	0.3107		
10	0.1936		
9	0.0907	0.3650	
8	**0.0056**	0.2291	
7	0.0722	0.1077	0.2997
6	0.1663	**0.0091**	0.1559
5	0.3000	0.0808	**0.0371**
4	0.4731	0.1989	0.0631
3	0.6580	0.3769	0.1920
2	0.8134	0.5987	0.3991
1	0.9100	0.8014	0.6601
0	0.9496	0.9222	0.8730
Near Optimum Plan	**(94,8)**	**(65,6)**	**(48,5)**

(Figures in bold face indicate the minimum RSD)

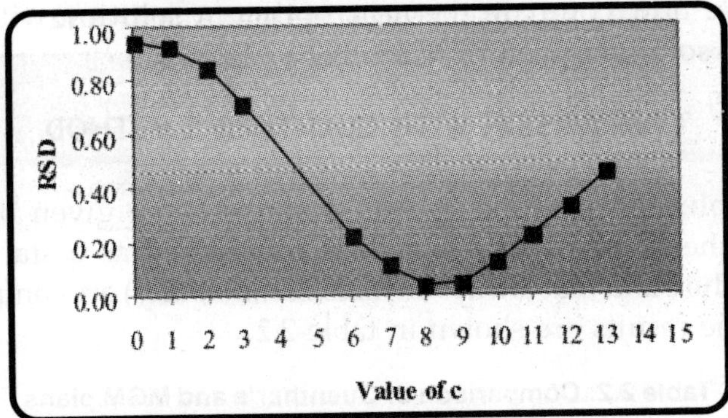

Fig. 2.3(a): Behaviour of RSD in Plan-4

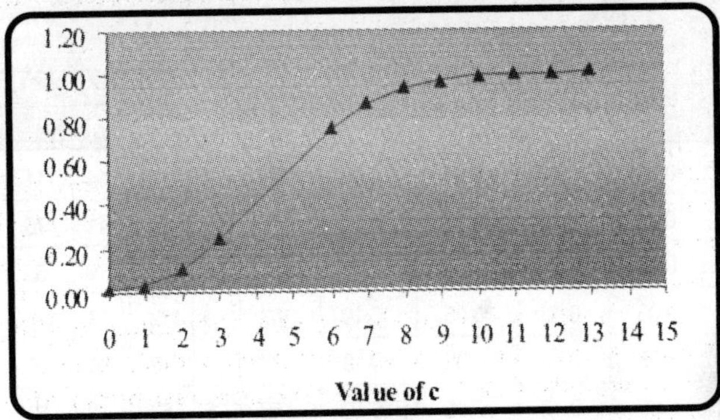

Fig. 2.3(b): Behaviour of error at AQL in Plan-4

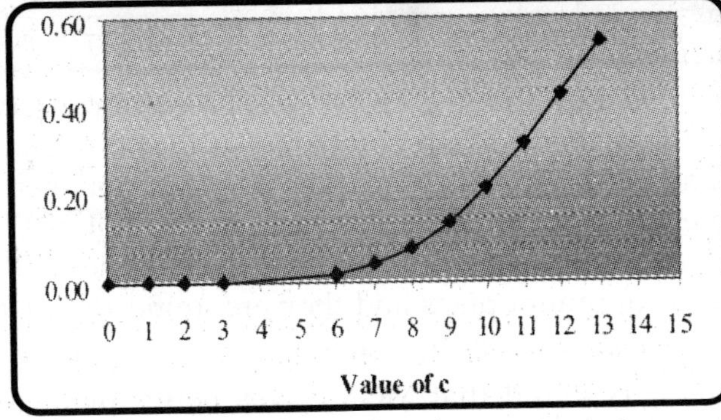

Fig. 2.3(c): Behaviour of error at RQL in Plan-4

We now compare the near optimum solution with the actual solution given by Guenther's algorithm.

COMPARISION WITH GUENTHER'S METHOD

The solution obtained by MGM and the one given by the Guenther's algorithm, (which is considered as a standard procedure and that always ensures admissibility) are compared and the results are shown in table-2.2.

Table 2.2: Comparison of Guenther's and MGM plans

Sl. No.	AQL	RQL	α	β	Guenther's Method		Graf *et al* Method		Modified Graf *et al* Method (MGM)	
					n	c	n_0	c_0	n_0	c_{opt}
1	0.05	0.13	0.05	0.08	120	10	111	14	111	9
2	0.05	0.15	0.05	0.08	79	7	76	11	76	7
3	0.05	0.17	0.05	0.08	62	6	56	9	56	5
4	0.05	0.13	0.05	0.10	107	9	102	13	102	8
5	0.05	0.15	0.05	0.10	77	7	70	10	70	6
6	0.05	0.17	0.05	0.10	53	5	52	8	52	5
7	0.05	0.13	0.05	0.12	95	8	94	11	94	8
8	0.05	0.15	0.05	0.12	66	6	65	9	65	6
9	0.05	0.17	0.05	0.12	51	5	48	7	48	5

It can be seen that the MGM offers a more conservative plan with smaller c when compared to that of Guenther's plan. The behaviour of OC curves of plans obtained from these methods for specific inputs AQL = 0.05, RQL = 0.13, α = 0.05 and β =0.1 is shown in figure-2.4. Thus the MGM has given near optimum plans and they are found to be close to the exact solution given by Guenther.

Thus it is found that MGM gives better plan (having smaller n) than Guenther's procedure with Binomial distribution. The earlier researchers have provided () FORTRAN programs to work with Guenther's procedure while we have developed a C-program for Guenther's procedure using both Binomial and Poisson cases.

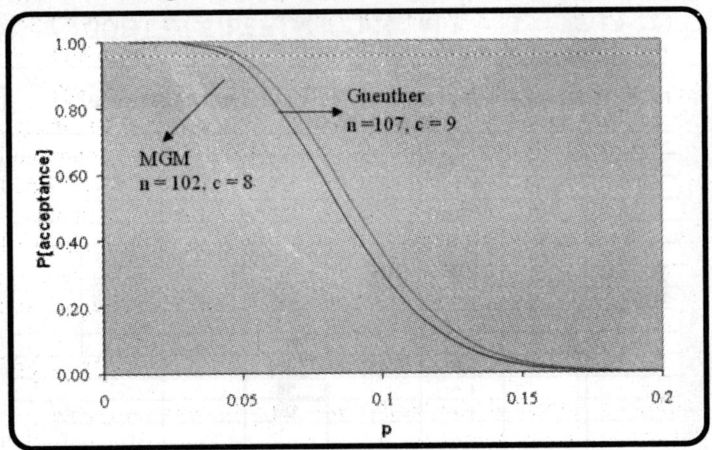

Fig. 2.4: Comparision of OC curves

In the following section a spreadsheet procedure for the Peach-Littauer's algorithm is developed and the results are compared with those obtained by Guenther's algorithm.

PEACH-LITTAUER'S ALGORITHM

The following are the steps of Peach-Littauer algorithm.

Step-1: Given values of AQL, RQL, α and β Calculate

$$q_1(c) = \frac{\chi^2_{2(c+1);1-\beta}}{2.RQL} \text{ and } q_2(c) = \frac{\chi^2_{2(c+1);\alpha}}{2.AQL} \text{ by taking c = 0.}$$

Step-2: Verify whether $q_1(c) \leq q_2(c)$. If it is satisfied, then n = smallest integer between $[q_1(c), q_2(c)]$; else go to next step.

Step-3: Increase c by one and repeat step-1 and step-2. The optimal solution corresponds to the n and c when the procedure terminates.

The above procedure can be implemented in Excel spreadsheet by using *Solver* which is given in figure-2.5.

Microsoft Excel - Peach

E14 =IF(D14=" ",(IF(F10<G10,D9," "))," ")

	A	B	C	D	E	F	G	H
1	EXCEL TEMPLATE FOR PEACH-LITTAUER'S ALGORITHM TO FIND n AND							
2	c USING SOLVER							
3	AQL =	0.05	DEN1=	0.26				
4	RQL =	0.13	DEN2=	0.10				
5	ALFA =	0.05	DEN1 =	0.26				
6	BETA =	0.08	1-ALFA=	0.95				
7								
8	NUM1	NUM2	C	C+1	2(C+1)	Q1(C)	Q2(C)	
9	29.40969	10.8508	9.50	10	20	113.1142	108.508	
10	31.849399	12.33801		11	22	122.4977	123.3801	
11								
12								
13			SINGLE SAMPLING PLAN					
14			c =		10			
15			n =		123			
16								
17								
18	VARIOUS STEPS WITH THIS EXCEL TEMPLATE							
19								
20	STEP1:CHANGE THE VALUES OF INPUTS LIKE AQL,RQL,ALFA,BETA IF REQUIRED							
21	STEP2:PUT CURSOR ON C9							
22	STEP3: RUN SOLVER							
23								

PEACH

Ready NUM

Fig. 2.5: Excel Template for implementing Peach-Littauer's algorithm

Illustration 2.2

Suppose AQL = 0.05, RQL = 0.13, *á* = 0.05 and *â* =0.08 then the Excel template gives n = 123 and c = 10 which exactly matches to the Guenther's solution. The plans for different input parameters are shown in table-2.3.

It can be seen from the above table that the sampling plan by Guenther's algorithm with Poisson OC and the plan given by the Peach-Littauer are *identical* for different values the input parameters. Peach-Littauer solution is obtained by a spreadsheet template, which is easy to implement than the Guenther's model to be run with C-program.

Table-2.3: Comparison of Guenther's and Peach-Littauer's plans

Sl.	AQL	RQL	α	β	Guenther (Poisson)		Peach-Littauer (Poisson)	
					n	c	n	c
1.	0.05	0.13	0.05	0.08	123	10	123	10
2.	0.05	0.15	0.05	0.08	90	8	90	8
3.	0.05	0.17	0.05	0.08	65	6	65	6
4.	0.05	0.13	0.05	0.10	119	10	119	10
5.	0.05	0.15	0.05	0.10	79	7	79	7
6.	0.05	0.17	0.05	0.10	62	6	62	6
7.	0.05	0.13	0.05	0.12	107	9	107	9
8.	0.05	0.15	0.05	0.12	76	7	76	7
9.	0.05	0.17	0.05	0.12	60	6	60	6

A SINGLE SAMPLING PLAN THAT MINIMIZES ATI

This type of plans can be derived for rectifying inspection with given values of fraction defective (p) and the lot size (N). The plan should pass through either the point (RQL,β) or (AQL,1-α). The general procedure to work with this method is explained below:

Step-1: Find the value of Poisson parameter np_β corresponding to β with $c = 0$.

This can be found by using the Excel function CHIINV().

Step-2: Find value of n using $n = np_\beta/\text{RQL}$.

Step-3: Find $\lambda = np$ for given p.

Step-4: Calculate OC (P_a) value for λ and c (=0) using POISSON (X, Mean, 1).

Step-5: Using this p_a compute ATI = $n + (N-n)(1-P_a)$

Step-6: Put $c = c+1$ and repeat the above steps until ATI attains minimum. Since ATI is convex in c, a unique minimum exists.

This is an iterative procedure that can be implemented in the Excel template, which is given in Figure-2.6 (*See on next page*).

Illustration-2.3

Let us take RQL = 0.10, β = 0.08, p = 0.02 and N = 1000. The above procedure yields the results shown in table-2.4.

Table-2.4: Parameters of SSP that minimizes ATI

c	np_β	n	$\lambda = np$	P_a	$1-P_a$	ATI
0.	2.3026	29	0.58	0.5599	0.4401	456
1.	3.8897	49	0.98	0.7431	0.2569	293
2.	5.3223	67	1.34	0.8478	0.1522	209
3.	6.6808	84	1.68	0.9098	0.0902	167
4.	7.9936	100	2.00	0.9473	0.0527	147
5.	9.2747	**116**	2.32	0.9689	0.0311	**143**
6.	10.5321	132	2.64	0.9815	0.0185	148
7.	11.7709	148	2.96	0.9889	0.0111	157
8.	12.9947	163	3.26	0.9936	0.0064	168
9.	14.2060	178	3.56	0.9963	0.0037	181
10.	15.4066	193	3.86	0.9978	0.0022	195

The *solver tool* automatically stops at c = 5. To show that ATI is convex, we have evaluated ATI for values beyond c = 5. The behaviour of ATI is shown in figure-2.7 (*See on next page*).

Microsoft Excel - Ati

File Edit View Insert Format Tools Data Window Help

H9

	A	B	C	D	E	F	G	H
1	EXCEL TEMPLATE TO DESIGN SSP WHICH MINIMIZES ATI USING SOLVER							
2								
3	Beta=	0.1	p =	0.02				
4	RQL=	0.08	N =	1000				
5	4.499999							
6	c	np(beta)	n	Lembda	1-pa	ATI		
7	4	7.9936	100	2.00	0.0527	147		
8	5	9.2747	116	2.32	0.0311	143		
9								
10		SINGLE SAMPLING PLAN						
11		Sample size(n) =		116				
12		Critical number(c) =		5				
13		Mnimum ATI =		143				
14								
15	STEPS INVOLVED IN THIS TEMPLATE							
16								
17	STEP-1: CHANGE INPUT VALUES LIKE BETA, RQL, p AND N IF REQUIRED.							
18	STEP-2: PUT CURSOR ON THE CELL A5.							
19	STEP-3: TOOLS>SOLVER>SOLVE(Then we can see reuslts in D11,D12 and D13)							

Sheet1 Sheet3

Ready NUM

Fig. 2.6: Excel template to design SSP that minimizes ATI

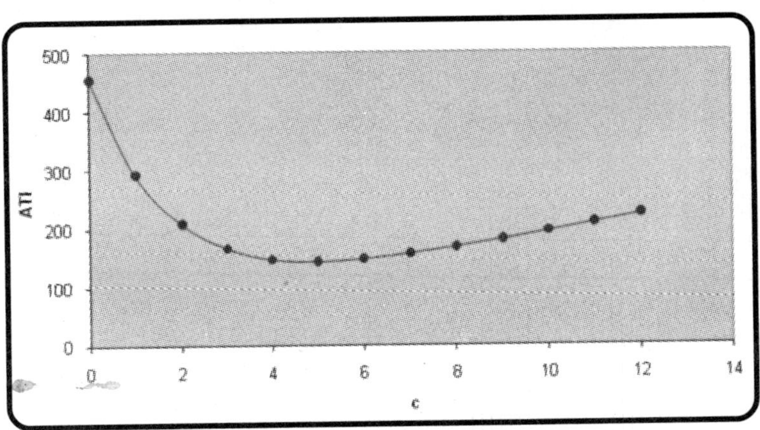

Fig. 2.7: Behaviour of ATI

Observations

In this chapter we have dealt with some aspects relating to the design of a single sampling plan. First we have shown that the algorithm-based procedures can be alternatively implemented in Excel worksheet by utilizing the statistical functions. It is observed that iterative procedures leading to the design of single sampling plan could be easily implemented in Excel spreadsheet with *solver tool*. This would reduce programming effort and helps in simulation experiments.

In the following chapter some aspects of Skip Lot Sampling Plans are considered in the light of the spreadsheet procedures.

On Some Computational Experiences with Skip-lot Sampling Plan

DETERMINATION OF SkSP PARAMETERS

The determination of the parameters of SkSP is linked to the parameters of SSP which is used as the reference plan. The performance of SkSP for given values of i and f have been studied by several authors (Dodge & Perry[10] (1971)) and tables were prepared. The OC and AFI depend on the acceptance probability of the reference plan. In this chapter we attempt to examine the effect of optimal SSP derived from MGM, on the performance parameters of the SkSP.

The following are two methods for deriving SkSP parameters i and k where $k = 1/f$.

Method-1

Specifying the average length of the 100 per cent inspection period

(u^*) and the average length of the f.100 per cent inspection period (v^*) for a given quality level P^*. Here P^* denotes the OC of the reference plan.

The parameters i and k can be determined by using the following formulae

$$i = \frac{In(u^*.P^*+1)}{In(1-P^*)} \text{ and} \tag{3.1a}$$

$$k = P^*.\, v^* \tag{3.2b}$$

The sensitivity of the above two formulae with respect to u^*, v^* and P^* can easily be observed by running these formulae in Excel sheet.

Method-2

Specifying two points on the OC curve at AQL and RQL.

This method is similar to that of the Guenther's procedure for designing single sampling plan for attributes. By giving two points on OC curve like ($P_{1-}\alpha$, 1-α) and (P_β, β), we find the values of i and k so as to satisfying admissibility conditions.

$L(P_{1-}\alpha \mid i; k) \geq 1\text{-}\alpha$ and $L(P_\beta \mid i; k) \leq \beta$

This requires an iterative procedure since the above two conditions lead to two interdependent non-linear equations. We introduce a different Spreadsheet procedure in which for a given value of i, suitable value of k (and hence $f = 1/k$) can be determined so as to meet the admissibility conditions as closely as possible. We can provide a limiting accuracy like ε for the closeness of error for meeting the admissibility conditions. It means the solution will be accepted if

$$| L(P_{1-}\alpha \mid i; k) - (1\text{-}\alpha) \mid \leq \varepsilon \text{ or} \tag{3.2a}$$

$$| L(P_\beta \mid i; k) - \beta \mid \varepsilon. \tag{3.2b}$$

These conditions can be implemented in the Solver module of Excel and the procedure converges in a few iterations. By specifying ε we are admitting a level of relaxation in meeting the conditions. However for certain parameters, the *Solver* procedure may find the true admissible solution while in some cases the procedure leads to a warning 'solver could not find a feasible solution'. It is enough to use ε only in such cases. The Excel template to carry out entire procedure is given in figure-3.1.

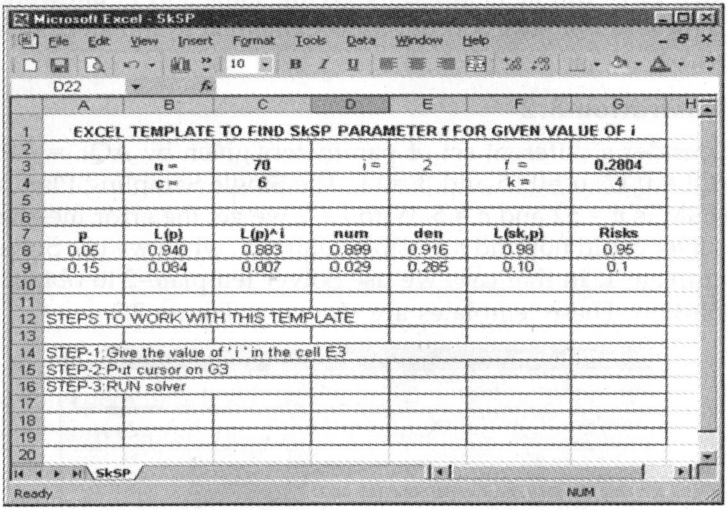

	A	B	C	D	E	F	G
1	EXCEL TEMPLATE TO FIND SkSP PARAMETER f FOR GIVEN VALUE OF i						
2							
3		n =	70	i =	2	f =	0.2804
4		c =	6			k =	4
5							
6							
7	p	L(p)	L(p)^i	num	den	L(sk,p)	Risks
8	0.05	0.940	0.883	0.899	0.916	0.98	0.95
9	0.15	0.084	0.007	0.029	0.285	0.10	0.1
10							
11							
12	STEPS TO WORK WITH THIS TEMPLATE						
13							
14	STEP-1: Give the value of 'i' in the cell E3						
15	STEP-2: Put cursor on G3						
16	STEP-3: RUN solver						

Fig. 3.1: Excel template to find *k* for given *i*

Consider the following illustration.

Illustration-3.1

Given AQL = 0.05, RQL= 0.15, α =0.05 and β =0.1, the Single Sampling Plan by MGM is n = 70 and c = 6. By using these values along with i = 2 as inputs we get k = 4 by running template-2. For this plan $L_{sk}(p)$ at AQL = 0.982 > 1-α and $L_{sk}(p)$ at RQL = 0.1 which is exactly equal to β. Hence this is an admissible plan.

Similarly with i = 3 we get k = 32 and for i = 4 we get k = 367. It means for the given reference plan with AQL of 5% and RQL of 15%, if 4 consecutive non defective lots are found, we can switch over to sampling with such a small fraction f = 0.0027. It means it is enough to inspect one out of 367 lots. Like wise we get k = 4365 and k= 10240 for i = 5 and i = 6 respectively. By this we can obverse that, a unit of increase in the value of *i* causes a rapid increase in value of *k*.

For certain values of the input parameters the solver iterations may not converge and an error message is displayed. Such cases can be handled by giving some sort of allowance in the admissibility conditions as explained in illustration-3.2 below.

Illustration-3.2

Consider a different set of parameters given by AQL = 0.05, RQL= 0.17, α =0.05 and β =0.1. The Single Sampling Plan by MGM is n = 52 and c = 5. With i = 2 we get the error message 'solver could not find a feasible solution', when we use Solver template-1. In that case we use Solver template-2 to obtain a solution. These templates are shown in Figure-3.2.

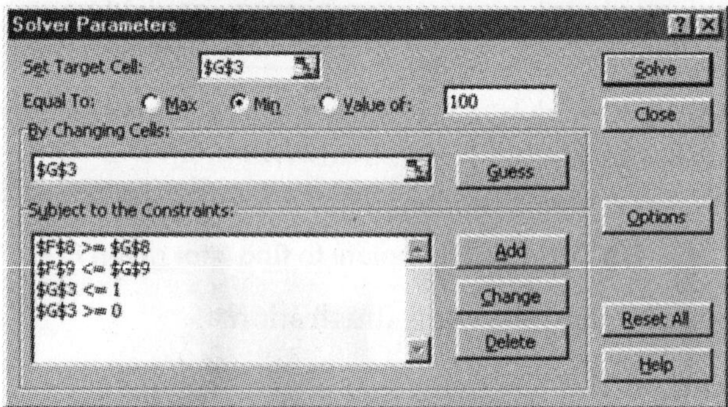

Fig. 3.2(a): Solver template-1

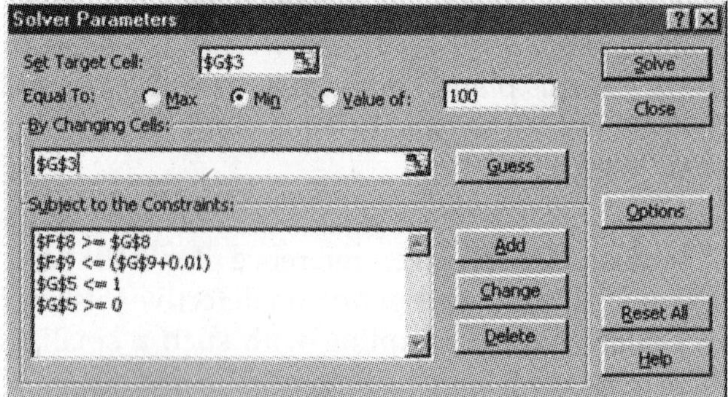

Fig. 3.2(b): Solver template-2

By replacing the condition F9 <= G9 with F9<= G9+0.01 an allowance is given in the condition meeting the type-2 risk β. Such an allowance may also be given even as F8 >= G8 if the OC value is already close to the admissible level at RQL. Using this type of relaxation gives the value of $k = 4$ at $i = 2$.

Thus a near-admissible plan can be found from Excel sheet without referring to statistical tables.

THE EFFECT OF REFERENCE PLAN ON THE OC OF SkSP

The properties of SkSP with different reference plans are discussed in this section.

The probability of accepting a lot under SkSP partly depends on the probability of lot acceptance under the reference plan. For each value of p, the difference $D = \{L_{sk}(p) - L(p)\}$ is evaluated. It is seen that the difference has increased with p until $p = 0.09$ and started to decrease. Any change in the input parameters of the MGM Template given in figure-2.1 of chapter-2 and for any change in parameter 'i' in SkSP template given in figure-3.1 can carry the corresponding changes in template given in table-3.1 of the SkSP.

We can observe the variations in the performance measures of SkSP with respect to changes in input parameters. Further with a given set of parameters, the sampling plan obtained by Guenther's algorithm and the one obtained by MGM can differ from each and as a result the performance of SkSP also varies.

According to Perry[31,32] (1973), the SkSP should satisfy $L_{sk}(p) \geq L(p)$ where $L(p)$ is the probability of accepting a lot under the reference plan. This condition is verified in both cases when the reference pan is taken from MGM and Guenther.

The OC and ASN functions of SkSP with these two reference plans are shown in table-3.3(a) and 3.3(b) respectively.

It follows from the above results that the MGM method is a good approximation to the Guenther's method. Further the ASN obtained by the MGM plan. is smaller than that of Guenther's reference plan.

Table-3.1: Effect of MGM as reference plan on SkSP

Reference Plan Parameters: AQL= 0.05, RQL= 0.13, α = 0.05, β = 0.08 Reference Plan: n =111, c = 9 SkSP plan parameters: i = 3, f = 0.0885						
p	L(p)	$L_{sk}(p)$	AFI	ASN	AOQ	$D=L_{sk}(p)-L(p)$
0.01	1.000	1.000	0.089	9	0.0100	0.000
0.03	0.998	1.000	0.089	9	0.0300	0.002
0.05	0.948	0.995	0.102	11	0.0497	0.046
0.07	0.750	0.953	0.187	20	0.0667	0.203
0.09	0.453	0.721	0.510	56	0.0649	0.268
0.11	0.209	0.277	0.914	101	0.0305	0.068
0.13	0.076	0.080	0.996	110	0.0104	0.004
0.15	0.022	0.023	1.000	110	0.0034	0.000
0.17	0.006	0.006	1.000	110	0.0009	0.000
0.19	0.001	0.001	1.000	110	0.0002	0.000
0.21	0.000	0.000	1.000	110	0.0000	0.000

Table 3.2: Effect of Guenther's plan as reference plan on SkSP

Reference Plan Parameters: AQL= 0.05, RQL= 0.13, α = 0.05, β = 0.08 Reference Plan: n =120, c = 10 SkSP plan parameters: i = 3, f = 0.1419						
p	L(p)	$L_{sk}(p)$	AFI	ASN	AOQ	$D=L_{sk}(p)-L(p)$
1	2	3	4	5	6	7
0.01	1.000	1.000	0.142	17	0.0100	0.000
0.03	0.999	1.000	0.142	17	0.0300	0.001
0.05	**0.962**	**0.994**	0.157	18	0.0497	0.032

(Contd...)

1	2	3	4	5	6	7
0.07	0.781	0.943	0.258	30	0.0660	0.163
0.09	0.479	0.688	0.600	72	0.0619	0.208
0.11	0.220	0.267	0.940	112	0.0293	0.047
0.13	**0.077**	**0.080**	0.997	119	0.0104	0.003
0.15	0.022	0.022	1.000	119	0.0033	0.000
0.17	0.005	0.005	1.000	119	0.0008	0.000
0.19	0.001	0.001	1.000	119	0.0002	0.000
0.21	0.000	0.000	1.000	119	0.0000	0.000

Table 3.3(a): OC values of MGM plan and Guenther's plan

p	$L_{SK}(p)$-(MGM)	$L_{SK}(p)$-(Guenther)	Deviation
0.01	1.000	1.000	0.000
0.03	1.000	1.000	0.000
0.05	0.995	0.994	0.001
0.07	0.953	0.943	0.010
0.09	0.721	0.688	0.033
0.11	0.277	0.267	0.010
0.13	0.080	0.080	0.000
0.15	0.023	0.022	0.001
0.17	0.006	0.005	0.001
0.19	0.001	0.001	0.000
0.21	0.000	0.000	0.000

Table-3.3(b): ASN values of MGM plan and Guenther's plan

p	ASN-(MGM)	ASN-(Guenther)	Deviation
1	2	3	4
0.01	9	17	-8
0.03	9	17	-8

(Contd...)

1	2	3	4
0.05	11	18	-7
0.07	20	30	-10
0.09	56	72	-16
0.11	101	112	-11
0.13	110	119	-9
0.15	110	119	-9
0.17	110	119	-9
0.19	110	119	-9
0.21	110	119	-9

BEHAVIOUR OF AOQL OF SkSP WITH DIFFERENT INPUTS

Given the reference plan, one would like to design the SkSP such that the plan has a specified AOQL. The input parameters like AQL, RQL, α and β of the reference plan would influence the AOQL. In this section an experimental study is taken up to workout the AOQL for different combinations of *i* and *f* with the help of Excel templates developed in this chapter.

The experimental data contains 3 sets of results with values fixed values of AQL = 0.05, α = 0.05. A single sampling plan as reference plan is generated by the MGM and it gives *n* and *c*.

For selected values of *i* and *f* of the SkSP the AOQL has been obtained and the results are shown in table-3.4(*a*), 3.4(*b*) and 3.4(c) from which the following observations can be made.

1. Keeping other parameters fixed, the values of n and c decrease as RQL increases. It means that higher the lot tolerance percent defective, we can use a sampling plan with small value of *n*. The situation is shown in figure-3.4(*a*) (*See on page 54*).
2. Keeping RQL fixed, the AOQL is found be non linear in β as shown in figure-3.4(*b*) (*See on page 54*).

Table-3.4(a): AOQL Values of SkSP with different parameters

i	AOQL of SkSP (MGM) for AQL = 0.05, α = 0.05, β = 0.08														
	RQL = 0.13, n = 111, c = 9					RQL = 0.15, n = 76, c = 7					RQL = 0.17, n = 56, c = 5				
	f =1/2	f =1/3	f =1/4	f =1/5	f =2/3	f =1/2	f =1/3	f =1/4	f =1/5	f =2/3	f =1/2	f =1/3	f =1/4	f =1/5	f =2/3
2	0.057	0.062	0.065	0.067	0.054	0.067	0.070	0.072	0.076	0.064	0.065	0.069	0.072	0.076	0.062
3	0.055	0.058	0.061	0.063	0.054	0.065	0.068	0.071	0.072	0.063	0.063	0.067	0.069	0.071	0.060
4	0.055	0.056	0.057	0.059	0.054	0.064	0.067	0.069	0.070	0.062	0.062	0.065	0.067	0.069	0.059
5	0.055	0.056	0.057	0.057	0.054	0.063	0.066	0.067	0.069	0.061	0.060	0.063	0.065	0.067	0.059
6	0.055	0.056	0.057	0.057	0.054	0.062	0.064	0.066	0.067	0.061	0.060	0.062	0.063	0.065	0.058
7	0.054	0.056	0.056	0.057	0.053	0.061	0.063	0.065	0.066	0.060	0.059	0.060	0.062	0.063	0.058
8	0.054	0.055	0.056	0.057	0.053	0.061	0.062	0.064	0.065	0.060	0.058	0.060	0.061	0.062	0.058
9	0.054	0.055	0.056	0.056	0.053	0.060	0.062	0.063	0.063	0.060	0.058	0.059	0.060	0.060	0.057
10	0.054	0.055	0.056	0.056	0.053	0.060	0.061	0.062	0.063	0.060	0.058	0.058	0.059	0.060	0.057
11	0.054	0.055	0.055	0.056	0.053	0.060	0.061	0.061	0.062	0.059	0.057	0.058	0.058	0.059	0.057
12	0.053	0.054	0.055	0.056	0.053	0.060	0.060	0.061	0.061	0.059	0.057	0.058	0.058	0.058	0.057

Table 3.4(b): AOQL Values of SkSP with different parameters

i	AOQL of SkSP (MGM) for AQL = 0.05, α = 0.05, β = 0.01														
	RQL = 0.13, n = 102, c = 8					RQL = 0.15, n = 70, c = 6					RQL = 0.17, n = 52, c = 5				
	f=1/2	f=1/3	f=1/4	f=1/5	f=2/3	f=1/2	f=1/3	f=1/4	f=1/5	f=2/3	f=1/2	f=1/3	f=1/4	f=1/5	f=2/3
2	0.054	0.056	0.063	0.058	0.053	0.062	0.066	0.069	0.071	0.059	0.069	0.075	0.079	0.082	0.066
3	0.054	0.056	0.058	0.057	0.053	0.060	0.064	0.066	0.068	0.057	0.067	0.070	0.073	0.076	0.065
4	0.054	0.055	0.056	0.057	0.052	0.058	0.062	0.064	0.066	0.056	0.066	0.069	0.071	0.072	0.064
5	0.053	0.055	0.056	0.056	0.052	0.057	0.060	0.062	0.063	0.056	0.065	0.068	0.070	0.071	0.063
6	0.053	0.054	0.055	0.056	0.052	0.056	0.058	0.060	0.061	0.055	0.064	0.067	0.068	0.070	0.063
7	0.053	0.054	0.055	0.056	0.052	0.055	0.057	0.058	0.059	0.055	0.064	0.066	0.067	0.068	0.063
8	0.052	0.054	0.055	0.055	0.052	0.055	0.056	0.057	0.058	0.054	0.063	0.065	0.066	0.067	0.062
9	0.052	0.053	0.054	0.055	0.051	0.055	0.055	0.056	0.057	0.054	0.063	0.064	0.065	0.066	0.062
10	0.052	0.053	0.054	0.054	0.051	0.054	0.055	0.056	0.056	0.054	0.063	0.064	0.065	0.653	0.062
11	0.052	0.053	0.053	0.054	0.051	0.054	0.055	0.056	0.056	0.054	0.062	0.063	0.064	0.065	0.062
12	0.052	0.052	0.053	0.054	0.051	0.054	0.055	0.055	0.056	0.054	0.062	0.063	0.063	0.064	0.062

Table 3.4(c): AOQL Values of SkSP with different Parameters

i	AOQL of SkSP (MGM) for AQL = 0.05, α = 0.05, β = 0.12														
	RQL = 0.13, n = 94, c = 8					RQL = 0.15, n = 65, c = 6					RQL = 0.17, n = 48, c = 5				
	f =1/2	f =1/3	f =1/4	f =1/5	f =2/3	f =1/2	f =1/3	f =1/4	f =1/5	f =2/3	f =1/2	f =1/3	f =1/4	f =1/5	f =2/3
2	0.061	0.066	0.068	0.070	0.058	0.066	0.070	0.074	0.077	0.064	0.076	0.081	0.085	0.087	0.071
3	0.059	0.063	0.066	0.068	0.056	0.065	0.068	0.071	0.072	0.063	0.073	0.078	0.081	0.084	0.070
4	0.057	0.061	0.063	0.065	0.055	0.064	0.067	0.069	0.070	0.062	0.071	0.075	0.078	0.080	0.068
5	0.056	0.059	0.060	0.062	0.055	0.063	0.065	0.067	0.069	0.061	0.069	0.072	0.074	0.077	0.068
6	0.056	0.057	0.058	0.060	0.055	0.062	0.064	0.066	0.067	0.061	0.069	0.071	0.072	0.074	0.067
7	0.055	0.056	0.057	0.058	0.055	0.061	0.063	0.065	0.066	0.060	0.068	0.070	0.072	0.073	0.067
8	0.055	0.056	0.056	0.057	0.054	0.061	0.062	0.063	0.065	0.060	0.068	0.070	0.071	0.072	0.067
9	0.055	0.056	0.057	0.057	0.054	0.060	0.061	0.062	0.063	0.060	0.067	0.069	0.070	0.071	0.067
10	0.055	0.056	0.057	0.057	0.054	0.060	0.061	0.062	0.062	0.060	0.067	0.068	0.070	0.070	0.066
11	0.055	0.056	0.056	0.057	0.054	0.060	0.060	0.061	0.062	0.059	0.067	0.068	0.069	0.070	0.066
12	0.055	0.056	0.056	0.057	0.054	0.060	0.060	0.061	0.610	0.059	0.067	0.068	0.068	0.069	0.066

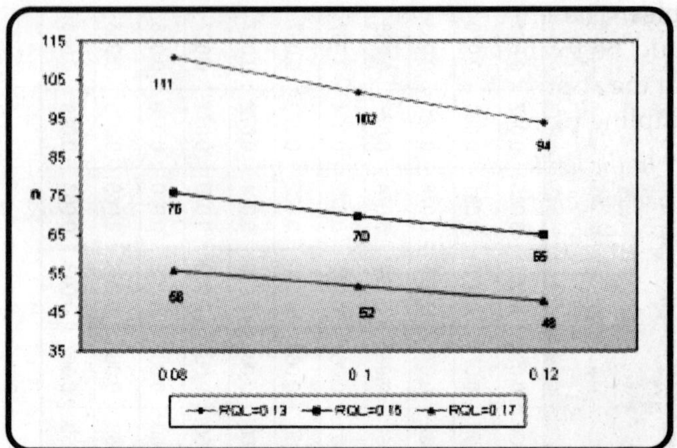

Fig. 3.4(a): Sample size of reference plan

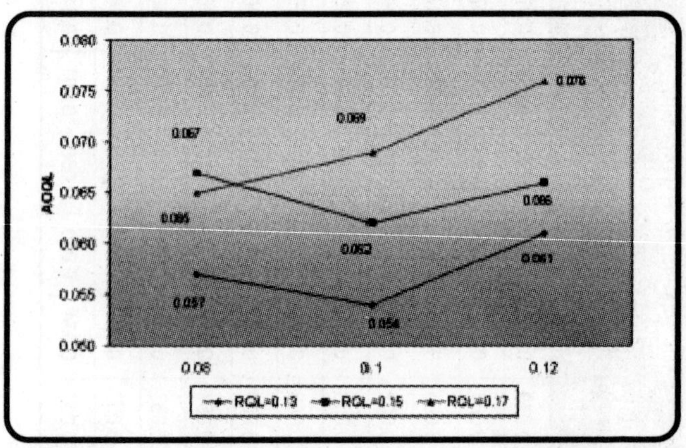

Fig. 3.4(b): AOQL of SkSP as a function of RQL

Observations

In this chapter we have derived a procedure to obtain a SkSP of the attribute type in which the reference plan is obtained by using a modified version of the Graf *et al* procedure. Using Excel Statistical functions and Solver module of MS-Excel we have obtained both reference plan and the SkSP from a single template. The advantage is that one need not refer to statistical tables. The effect of reference plan parameters on the SkSP could be examined on the Excel template itself. It is found that the approached used in this chapter gives a near optimum sampling plan.

In the next chapter discussion is made on the characterization of inspection errors and their influence on Single Sampling plan as well as Skip lot sampling plan.

Characterization of Inspection Errors and Their Effect on Skip Lot Sampling Plan

INSPECTION ERRORS AND THEIR BEHAVIOUR

Inspection Error is one aspect that influences the performance of a sampling plan. The problem of misclassification in case of attribute type inspection and measurement errors in case of variables is an interesting area. Greenberg and Stokes[15,16] (1995,1992) have studied the problem of repetitive testing in the presence of errors and also estimated the non-conformity rate after zero defect sampling with rectification. Anderson, Greenberg and Stokes[2] (2001) have considered the problem of estimation of number of non-conformities remaining in the outgoing lots after acceptance sampling with rectification when inspection errors occur. Some related work on these aspects can be found in Hahn[19](1986), Zaslavsky[42](1988). In the recent years there is growing interest in this area both by theoretical researchers as well as the industry.

When inspection errors are present in attribute inspection, the fraction defective will be distorted. The *apparent fraction defective* (AFD), which is rectified for errors gives true values of OC and ASN. It would be interesting to estimate the AFD by utilizing knowledge on the statistical behaviour of pattern of errors.

The inspection risks namely type-I and type-II risks denoted by ε and ϕ are assumed to take continuous such that $0 \leq (\varepsilon, \phi)d''$ 1 One can use Uniform distribution or Beta distribution of type-1 to explain the behaviour of these risks.

The expression for AFD as derived in (1.11) of chapter-1 is

$$\pi = p(1\text{-f}) + (1\text{-}p)\,\varepsilon \qquad (4.1)$$

where p is the incoming fraction defective.

When the inspector commits only type-I inspection error, the true fraction defective in the lot is *under-estimated* as p+(1-p)ε. If type-II inspection error alone is committed by the inspector the proportion of good items (1-p) in the lot is over-estimated as $p(1\text{-}\phi)$.

When the inspector changes the gage or inspector himself is changed from the testing station or when the operating environment gets disturbed, it is possible that the inspection risks are dragged to one of the extremes i.e., 0 or 1. In other words ε and ϕ both may come closer to 0 or 1.

It is therefore reasonable to describe the inspection risk as a continuous random variable Y, $0 \leq Y \leq 1$. We can use either Uniform distribution in [0,1] or Beta distribution of type-1 to describe the behaviour of Y. In a recent unpublished work Khader Babu (2003) has examined the effect of this distribution on the performance of Single Sampling Plan.

In practice the maximum risk is far less than unity and usually close to 0. So instead of a full range Beta distribution, it is appropriate to use truncated Beta distribution. We now examine the Beta distribution truncated at b <1.

THE SYMMETRIC BETA DISTRIBUTION TRUNCATED AT B (0 < B <1)

The probability density function (pdf) of Y following Beta distribution with parameters (m,n) is given by

$$g\ (y,\ m,\ n) = \frac{y^{m-1}(1-y)^{n-1}}{\beta(m,n)},\ 0 \le y \le 1 \text{ and } (m,\ n) \ge 1$$

where $\beta\ (m,\ n) = \dfrac{\Gamma(m)\Gamma(n)}{\Gamma(m+n)}$

When $n = m$, the Beta distribution will be symmetric around the mean. We use the notation $g(y \mid m,\ m)$ to denote this density given by

$$g\ (y,\ m,\ m) = \frac{y^{m-1}(1-y)^{m-1}}{\beta(m,m)},0 \le y \le 1 \text{ and } m \ge 1 \qquad (4.2)$$

where $\beta(m,m) = \dfrac{\Gamma(m)\Gamma(m)}{\Gamma(2m)}$

Let $0 < b < 1$ be a real number at which the Beta distribution is to be truncated.

Let I $(m,\ m,\ b) = \int_0^b y^{m-1}(1-y)^{m-1}$ dy be the incomplete Beta integral.

Then $P\ [0 \le Y \le b] = \dfrac{I(m,m,b)}{\beta(m,m)}$ so that that the truncated density of the Beta distribution becomes

$$g(y \mid m,m,b) = \frac{f(y)}{P(Y \le b)}$$

$$= \begin{cases} \dfrac{y^{m-1}(1-y)^{m-1}}{I(m,m,b)},0 \le y \le b \\ 0 \qquad\qquad \text{Otherwise} \end{cases}$$

Working with this density requires the values of incomplete Beta function. Using incomplete Beta tables or spreadsheet function in Excel we can evaluate the moments of this distribution. For this truncated density

$$E_b(Y) = \int_0^b \frac{y.y^{m-1}(1-y)^{m-1}}{I(m,m,b)} dy$$

$$= \int_0^b \frac{y^m(1-y)^{m-1}}{I(m,m,b)} dy$$

Using the relationship 1 $(m, n, b) = y.1\ (m, b)$ it follows that

$$E_b(Y) = \frac{1}{I(m,m,b)} I(m+1,m,b)$$

While a closed form expression is not possible, it is however possible to evaluate the moments of this distribution for specific values of m. Here are some particular cases.

Case-1: $m = 1$

$$g(y \mid 1,1,b) = \begin{cases} \frac{1}{b}, & 0 \le y \le b \\ 0 & \text{otherwise} \end{cases}$$

The mean and variance of this distribution are given by

$$E_b^{(1)}(Y) = \frac{b}{2} \tag{4.3a}$$

and $$V_b^{(1)}(Y) = \frac{b^2}{12}. \tag{4.3b}$$

The superscript for the moments indicates the value of m.

Case-2: $m = 2$

The density becomes

$$g(y \mid 2,2,b) = \begin{cases} \frac{6y(1-y)}{3b^2 - 2b^3}, 0 \le y \le b \\ 0 \qquad \text{Otherwise} \end{cases}$$

The mean and variance are respectively given by

$$E_b^{(2)}(Y) = \frac{4b - 3b^2}{6 - 4b} \tag{4.4a}$$

and

$$V_b^{(2)}(Y) = \left[\frac{15b^2 - 12b^3}{30 - 20b}\right] - \left[\frac{4b - 3b^2}{6 - 4b}\right]^2 \tag{4.4b}$$

Case 3: *m* = 3

The density becomes

$$g(y \mid 3,3,b) = \begin{cases} \dfrac{30y^2(1-y)^2}{\left(6b^5 - 15b^4 - 10b^3\right)}, 0 \le y \le b \\ 0 \qquad \text{Otherwise} \end{cases}$$

The mean and variance are respectively

$$E_b^{(3)}(Y) = \frac{10b^3 - 24b^2 + 15b}{12b^2 - 30b + 20} \tag{4.5a}$$

and

$$V_b^{(3)}(Y) = \left[\frac{30b^4 - 70b^3 + 42b^2}{42b^2 - 105b + 70}\right] - \left[\frac{10b^3 - 24b^2 + 15b}{12b^2 - 30b + 20}\right]^2 \tag{4.5b}$$

Case-4: *m* = 4

The density becomes

$$g(y \mid 4,4,b) = \begin{cases} \dfrac{140y^3(1-y)^3}{\left(35b^4 - 84b^5 + 70b^6 - 20b^7\right)}, 0 \le y \le b \\ 0 \qquad \text{Otherwise} \end{cases}$$

The mean and variance are respectively

$$E_b^{(4)}(Y) = \frac{168b - 420b^2 + 360b^3 - 105b^4}{210 - 504b + 420b^2 - 120b^3} \quad (4.6a)$$

and

$$V_b^{(4)}(Y) = \left[\frac{420b^2 - 1080b^3 + 945b^4 - 280b^5}{630 - 1512b + 1260b^2 - 360b^3}\right] - \left[\frac{168b - 420b^2 + 360b^3 - 105b^4}{210 - 504b + 420b^2 - 120b^3}\right]^2 \quad (4.6b)$$

In all the three cases when $b = 1$ the truncation will have no effect and the mean of the distribution reduces $E(Y) = ½$ but $V(Y)$ decreases as m increases.

For different values of the truncation point b, the mean and standard deviation have been worked out using the Excel worksheet and the results are shown in table- 4.1.

Table 4.1: Values of mean and standard deviation for truncated beta distribution

b	g(y|1,1,b)		g(y|2,2,b)		g(y|3,3,b)		g(y|4,4,b)	
	Mean	SD	Mean	SD	Mean	SD	Mean	SD
0.01	0.0050	0.00289	0.0067	0.00236	0.0075	0.00194	0.0080	0.00164
0.02	0.0100	0.00577	0.0133	0.00472	0.015	0.00389	0.0160	0.00328
0.03	0.0150	0.00866	0.0199	0.00709	0.0224	0.00584	0.0239	0.00494
0.04	0.0200	0.01155	0.0266	0.00945	0.0299	0.00780	0.0319	0.00660
0.05	0.0250	0.01443	0.0332	0.01182	0.0373	0.00976	0.0398	0.00827

The following observations can be made from the above values:

1. As b increases both the mean and standard deviation increase for selected combinations of m.
2. For a fixed value of b, an increase in m results in an increase in mean and a decrease in standard deviation.

We now use the truncated Beta distribution with parameters (1,1) , (2,2), (3,3) and (4,4) and examine its effect on the apparent fraction defective.

EXPECTED APPARENT FRACTION DEFECTIVE AND ITS BEHAVIOUR

When both ε and ϕ are truncated at the same value $0 \leq b < 1$, the apparent fraction defective can be worked out in a closed form. Consider the following cases.

Substituting the expressions for the mean from (4.3*a*), (4.4*a*) (4.5*a*) and (4.6*a*) in (4.1) gives the following expressions for the Expected AFD.

- $\pi_e^{(1)} = p(1-b) + 0.5b$, for $m = 1$

- $\pi_e^{(2)} = \dfrac{p\left(6-12b+6b^2\right)+\left(4b-3b^2\right)}{(6-4b)}$, for $m = 2$

- $\pi_e^{(3)} = \dfrac{p\left(20-60b+60b^2-20b^3\right)+\left(15b-24b^2+10b^3\right)}{\left(20-30b+12b^2\right)}$, for $m = 3$

- $\pi_e^{(4)} = \dfrac{p\left(210-840b+1260b^2-840b^3+210b^4\right)+\left(168b-420b^2+360b^3-105b^4\right)}{(210-504b+420b^2-120b^3)}$, for $m = 4$

The expressions for the Expected AFD for different truncation levels are exhibited in table-4.2.

It can be seen that Expected AFD is a linear function of p for a given value of b. As b increases, the intercept of the line is found to increase while the slope of the line decreases for all the cases of m = 1, 2,3 and 4.

Table 4.2: Expressions for the Expected AFD with different parameters

Truncation Level (b)	g(y| 1,1,b)	g(y| 2,2,b)
0.01	$\pi_e^{(1)} = 0.99p + 0.005$	$\pi_e^{(2)} = 0.9867p + 0.0067$
0.02	$\pi_e^{(1)} = 0.98p + 0.010$	$\pi_e^{(2)} = 0.9734p + 0.0133$
0.03	$\pi_e^{(1)} = 0.97p + 0.015$	$\pi_e^{(2)} = 0.9601p + 0.0199$
0.04	$\pi_e^{(1)} = 0.96p + 0.020$	$\pi_e^{(2)} = 0.9468p + 0.0266$
0.05	$\pi_e^{(1)} = 0.95p + 0.025$	$\pi_e^{(2)} = 0.9336p + 0.0332$
Truncation Level (b)	**g(y| 3,3,b)**	**g(y|4,4,b)**
0.01	$\pi_e^{(3)} = 0.9850p + 0.0075$	$\pi_e^{(4)} = 0.9840p + 0.0080$
0.02	$\pi_e^{(3)} = 0.9701p + 0.0150$	$\pi_e^{(4)} = 0.9681p + 0.0160$
0.03	$\pi_e^{(3)} = 0.9551p + 0.0224$	$\pi_e^{(4)} = 0.9521p + 0.0239$
0.04	$\pi_e^{(3)} = 0.9402p + 0.0299$	$\pi_e^{(4)} = 0.9363p + 0.0319$
0.05	$\pi_e^{(3)} = 0.9254p + 0.0373$	$\pi_e^{(4)} = 0.9204p + 0.0398$

Illustration 4.1: The behaviour of Expected AFD for selected values of p and b has been studied with parameters (1,1), (2,2), (3,3) and (4,4) and the results are shown in table-4.3(a) and table-4.3(b). The following observations can be made on the behaviour of AFD.

- At any given level of true fraction defective p, the AFD increase gradually as b increases. It means that if the maximum allowed error risk increases, the AFD will be quite different from the true fraction defective. For p = 0.03 and the errors are distributed as $\beta(1,1)$ the AFD became 0.0535 when b = 0.05 while it was only 0.0347 when b was 0.01. Similar pattern is found when the risk distribution is taken as $\beta(2,2)$, $\beta(3,3)$ and $\beta(4,4)$.

- For fixed values of p and b the AFD also shows an increase trend as m increase from 1 to 4.

Table 4.3(a): Expected Apparent Fraction Defectives for different *p* and *b*

p	Expected Apparent Fraction Defective using g(y|1,1,b)				
	0.01	0.02	0.03	0.04	0.05
0.01	0.0149	0.0198	0.0247	0.0296	0.0345
0.02	0.0248	0.0296	0.0344	0.0392	0.0440
0.03	0.0347	0.0394	0.0441	0.0488	0.0535
0.04	0.0446	0.0492	0.0538	0.0584	0.0630
0.05	0.0545	0.0590	0.0635	0.0680	0.0725
0.06	0.0644	0.0688	0.0732	0.0776	0.0820
0.07	0.0743	0.0786	0.0829	0.0872	0.0915

p	Expected Apparent Fraction Defective using g(y|2,2,b)				
	0.01	0.02	0.03	0.04	0.05
0.01	0.0165	0.0230	0.0296	0.0360	0.0425
0.02	0.0264	0.0328	0.0392	0.0455	0.0519
0.03	0.0363	0.0425	0.0488	0.0550	0.0612
0.04	0.0461	0.0522	0.0584	0.0644	0.0705
0.05	0.0560	0.0620	0.0680	0.0739	0.0799
0.06	0.0659	0.0717	0.0776	0.0834	0.0892
0.07	0.0757	0.0814	0.0872	0.0929	0.0985

Table 4.3(b): Expected Apparent Fraction Defectives for different *p* and *b*

p	Expected Apparent Fraction Defective using g(y|3,3,b)				
	0.01	0.02	0.03	0.04	0.05
1	2	3	4	5	6
0.01	0.0173	0.0247	0.0320	0.0393	0.0466
0.02	0.0272	0.0344	0.0415	0.0487	0.0558

(Contd...)

1	2	3	4	5	6
0.03	0.0370	0.0441	0.0511	0.0581	0.0651
0.04	0.0469	0.0538	0.0606	0.0675	0.0743
0.05	0.0567	0.0635	0.0702	0.0769	0.0836
0.06	0.0666	0.0732	0.0797	0.0863	0.0928
0.07	0.0764	0.0829	0.0893	0.0957	0.1021

p	Expected Apparent Fraction Defective using g(y|4,4,b)				
	0.01	0.02	0.03	0.04	0.05
0.01	0.0178	0.0256	0.0334	0.0412	0.0490
0.02	0.0277	0.0353	0.0430	0.0506	0.0582
0.03	0.0375	0.0450	0.0525	0.0600	0.0674
0.04	0.0474	0.0547	0.0620	0.0693	0.0766
0.05	0.0572	0.0644	0.0715	0.0787	0.0858
0.06	0.0670	0.0741	0.0811	0.0880	0.0950
0.07	0.0769	0.0837	0.0906	0.0974	0.1042

EMPIRICAL VALUES OF AQL AND RQL AND ERROR MEAN-ADJUSTED PLAN (EMAP)

When inspection errors are present the *AQL* and *RQL* also get distorted. For known values of ε and ϕ the empirical values of *AQL* and *RQL* will be

$$= AQL(1-\phi) + (1-AQL)\varepsilon \qquad 4.7(a)$$

$$= RQL(1-\phi) + (1-RQL)\varepsilon \qquad 4.7(b)$$

If the inspection error probabilities are not known exactly but their pattern of occurrence is known by means of a probability distribution, we can replace and ϕ with their expectations $E(\varepsilon)$ and $E(\phi)$ respectively. Then the Expressions for the empirical values of *AQL* and *RQL*, denoted by AQL^* and RQL^* become

$$AQL^* = AQL(1-E(\phi)) + (1-AQL)E(\varepsilon) \qquad 4.8(a)$$

$$RQL^* = RQL(1-E(\phi)) + (1-RQL)E(\varepsilon) \qquad 4.8(b)$$

Such a plan in which the AQL and RQL are corrected for errors is called *Error Adjusted Plan*. The refinement made here is replacing ε and ϕ with their expectations so that the resulting plan may be called *Error Mean-Adjusted Plan* (EMAP).

In the following section the performance of EMAP is compared with different parameters of Truncated Beta distribution.

EFFECT OF BETA DISTRIBUTED INSPECTION ERROR ON SINGLE SAMPLING PLAN WITH PARAMETERS M =2, M =3 AND M = 4

Reconsider the Single Sampling Plan with n = 111 and c = 9 from chapter-2 by using the MGM with input parameters AQL = 0.05, RQL = 0.13, α = 0.05 and β = 0.08 . When inspection errors are present with beta distributed pattern, the empirical values of AQL and RQL by using equations 4.8(a) and 4.8(b) are calculated and listed below for values of m =2,3,4 at the point of truncation b = 0.04.

m	AQL^*	RQL^*
1	0.0680	0.1448
2	0.0739	0.1479
3	0.0769	0.1521
4	0.0787	0.1536

Using the above empirical values along with the specified α and β, one can get the Single Sampling Plan (n, c) by MGM (chapter-2) as (155,17), (161,18) and (164,18) corresponding to m = 2, m = 3 and m = 4 respectively. The OC values of these plans are shown in table-4.4.

1. From the above values it follows that the Expected AFD increases as m increases for any given value of the incoming fraction defective p.
2. The probability of accepting a lot is found to decrease as m increase for a given level of p.

Table 4.4: OC values of different plans

Error free Plan AQL= 0.05 RQL= 0.13 n = 111, c = 9		Errors present with g(y|2,2,0.04) AQL*=0.0739 RQL*=0.1497 E(ε) = E(ϕ) = 0.0266 n =155, c =17		Errors present with g(y|3,3,0.04) AQL*=0.0769 RQL*=0.1521 E(ε)=E(ϕ) = 0.0299 n =161, c = 18		Errors present with g(y|4,4,0.04) AQL*=0.0787 RQL*=0.1536 E(ε)=E(ϕ) = 0.0319 n =164, c = 18	
p	L(p)	$p_e^{(2)}$	OC	$p_e^{(3)}$	OC	$p_e^{(4)}$	OC
0.01	1.0000	0.0360	1.0000	0.0393	1.0000	0.0412	0.9999
0.02	0.9999	0.0455	0.9997	0.0487	0.9997	0.0506	0.9993
0.03	0.9981	0.0550	0.9977	0.0581	0.9973	0.0600	0.9954
0.04	0.9862	0.0644	0.9886	0.0675	0.9873	0.0693	0.9804
0.05	0.9483	0.0739	0.9618	0.0769	0.9587	0.0787	0.9418
0.06	0.8699	0.0834	0.9041	0.0863	0.8985	0.0880	0.8671
0.07	0.7502	0.0929	0.8081	0.0957	0.7998	0.0974	0.7533
0.08	0.6040	0.1023	0.6783	0.1051	0.6678	0.1068	0.6108
0.09	0.4533	0.1118	0.5307	0.1145	0.5193	0.1161	0.4594
0.1	0.3179	0.1213	0.3858	0.1239	0.3747	0.1255	0.3200

3. Interestingly it can be noted that the OC value of the plan for $m = 4$ is close to the OC value of the error-free plan. This is partly due to the chosen truncation level $b = 0.04$.

4. With smaller values of m, the EMAP has a higher distinguishing ability between good and bad lots than the error free plan.

Suppose the AQL and RQL are not adjusted for error but p is adjusted for error. Then the resulting plan will be $n = 111$ and $c = 9$. This is error free plan. Since the same AQL and RQL are used the plan derived by MGM did not differ from this and we call it 'partially adjusted plan'. Here an interesting attempt is made on $g(y|3,3,0.04)$ which is Beta distribution truncated at $b = 0.04$. The comparative results are listed in the table-4.5.

Table 4.5: Values of OC with and without inspection errors

Plan-1		Plan-2		Plan-3	
Error Free Plan		Partially Adjusted Plan		Error Mean Adjusted Plan	
P	L(p)	$p_e^{(3)}$	$L(p_e^{(3)})$	$p_e^{(3)}$	$L_{EMAP}(p_e^{(3)})$
0.010	1.0000	0.0393	0.9877	0.0393	1.0000
0.020	0.9999	0.0487	0.9554	0.0487	0.9997
0.030	0.9981	0.0581	0.8883	0.0581	0.9973
0.040	0.9862	0.0675	0.7836	0.0675	0.9873
0.050	0.9483	0.0769	0.6510	0.0769	0.9587
0.060	**0.8699**	**0.0863**	**0.5083**	**0.0863**	**0.8985**
0.070	0.7502	0.0957	0.3734	0.0957	0.7998
0.080	0.6040	0.1051	0.2588	0.1051	0.6678
0.090	0.4533	0.1145	0.1698	0.1145	0.5193
0.100	0.3179	0.1239	0.1059	0.1239	0.3747

*The behaviour of these three plans is shown in figure-4.1.

From this table we can observe that:

- Plan-2 accepts less percentage of lots than plan-1 and plan-3 at any given p. This is because plan-2 is not fully corrected for inspection errors. It has used uncorrected AQL and RQL.
- The percentage of lots accepted by plan-3 is closer to that of plan-1 because this plan is corrected for p, AQL and RQL.
- Suppose p = 0.06, which means lots are expected to arrive with 6 per cent defectives. Then plan-3 accepts 89.9 per cent of lots where as plan-2 accepts 50.8 per cent and plan-1 accepts 87 per cent of lots.
- In plan-2 and plan-3 the effective fraction defective used is 0.0863 against the true value 0.06.

- The effect of inspection errors and its characterization is responsible for this behaviour. The distribution used, its parameters and the level of truncation are the major determinants of the error corrected plan.

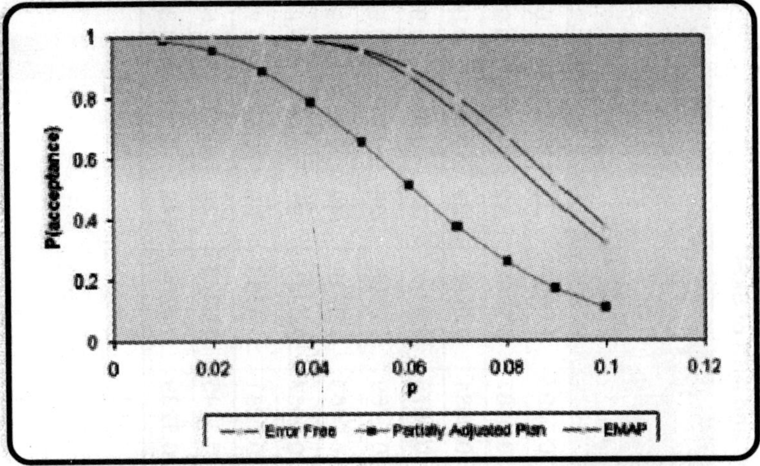

Fig. 4.1 : Values of OC with and without inspection errors

In the following section the performance of SkSP is investigated by considering EMAP derived from Beta distribution truncated at $b = 0.04$.

EFFECT OF INSPECTION ERROR ON SKIP-LOT SAMPLING PLAN

The effect of truncated Beta distributed inspection error on Skip-lot Sampling Plan is observed in this section by reconsidering the SSP with the help of MGM developed in chapter-2. For the sake of illustration we take parameters of SkSP-2 as $i = 4$ and $f = 0.2$ and reference plan is adjusted for errors using Beta distribution with different parameters truncated at $b = 0.04$. The results obtained are given in the table-4.6.

The following observations can be made from the above calculations.

Table 4.6: Values of OC and ASN of SkSP

Performance of SkSP with EMAP as reference plan : i = 4 and f = 0.2												
	Error free plan		g(y|2,2,0.04)			g(y|3,3,0.04)			g(y|4,4,0.04)			
p	$L_{sk}(p)$	ASN	$\pi_e^{(2)}$	$L_{sk}(\pi_e^{(2)})$	ASN	$\pi_e^{(3)}$	$L_{sk}(\pi_e^{(3)})$	ASN	$\pi_e^{(4)}$	$L_{sk}(\pi_e^{(4)})$	ASN
0.010	1.0000	22	0.0360	1.0000	31	0.0393	1.0000	32	0.0412	1.0000	32
0.020	1.0000	22	0.0455	0.9999	31	0.0487	0.9999	32	0.0506	0.9999	32
0.030	0.9996	22	0.0550	0.9995	31	0.0581	0.9995	32	0.0600	0.9991	33
0.040	0.9971	23	0.0644	0.9976	32	0.0675	0.9974	33	0.0693	0.9958	34
0.050	0.9878	26	0.0739	0.9914	35	0.0769	0.9906	36	0.0787	0.9860	39
0.060	0.9605	33	0.0834	0.9739	42	0.0863	0.9718	44	0.0880	0.9593	50
0.070	0.8898	48	0.0929	0.9291	57	0.0957	0.9241	61	0.0974	0.8922	71
0.080	0.7415	72	0.1023	0.8258	83	0.1051	0.8150	89	0.1068	0.7499	105
0.090	0.5323	94	0.1118	0.6437	117	0.1145	0.6276	124	0.1161	0.5412	139
0.100	0.3447	106	0.1213	0.4358	142	0.1239	0.4204	149	0.1255	0.3474	157

The OC and ASN functions are shown graphically in figure-4.2(*a*) and 4.2(*b*) respectively.

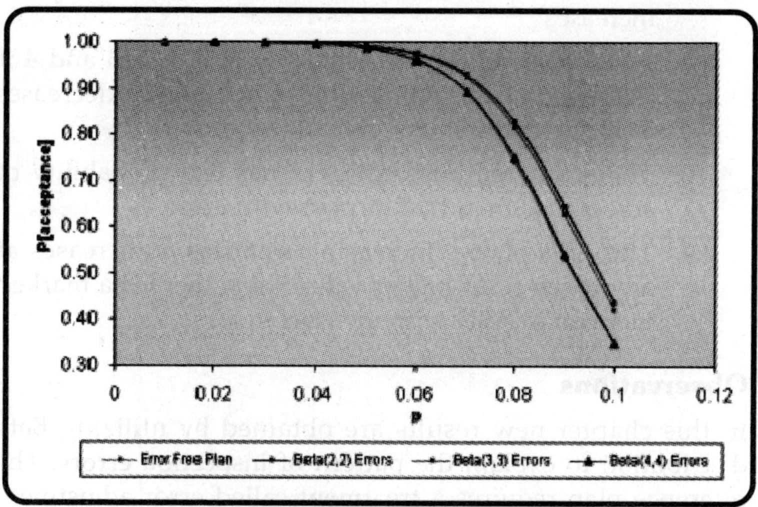

Fig. 4.2(*a*): OC of SkSP with and without inspection errors

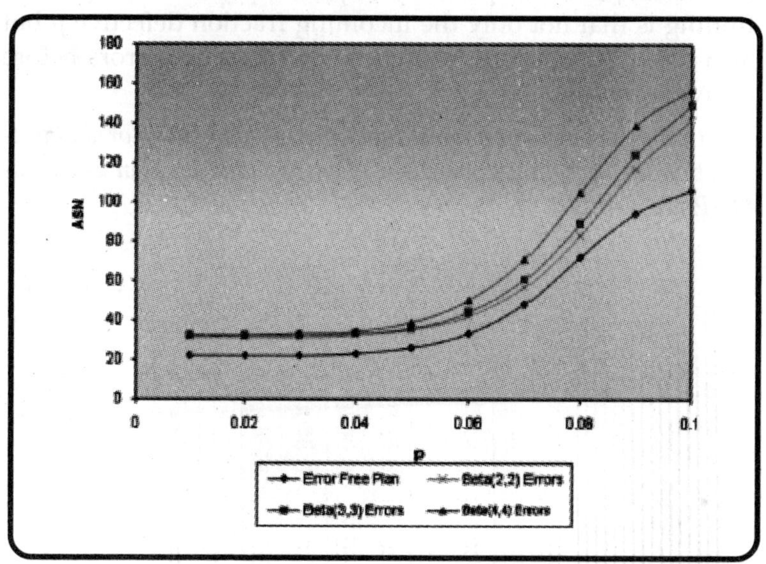

Fig. 4.2(*b*): ASN of SkSP with and without inspection errors

1. At any given value of p, the Apparent Fraction Defective is found to increase as the value of m increases
2. By comparing the OC values with m = 2 ,3 and 4 it follows that the probability of acceptance decreases as m increases at any given level of p.
3. The error free plan however has less probability of acceptance than that of plan with error.
4. The ASN shows increasing trend as m increases at any given p. At higher values of p, there is a marked increase in ASN with increase in m.

Observations

In this chapter new results are obtained by utilizing Beta distribution to explain the pattern of inspection errors. The reference plan requires a treatment called error adjustment and it is found that the EMAP provides a steeper OC curve than unadjusted or partially adjusted plan. The important finding is that not only the incoming fraction defective p but also the AQL and RQL should be corrected for errors before deriving the plan.

In the next chapter a novel type of inspection is explored and its effect on the acceptance procedure of singe sampling plan as well as SkSP are outlined.

A NEW TYPE OF INSPECTION

In SkSP-1 every lot is considered as one unit having a material of homogenous quality. The lot is accepted or rejected using CSP-1 basing on a lab test. This procedure is applicable for bulk sampling of lots containing raw materials such as fluids, rubbles, gases etc. The basic assumption is that the quality remains uniform within the lot. In practice this assumption may not be true when materials are supplied by vendors whose quality history shows unstable performance. Here is a case of an oil expeller who extracts non-edible oil from rice-bran.

Case: Rice bran is supplied by the vendors in bags each containing 50 kilos. The vendor procures rice bran from different rice mills where paddy of different varieties is milled. The oil manufacturer, on receiving the consignment, finds that the oil content from the bran is not uniform within as well as between the bags. Quantity is tested on a sample of bran drawn at random from the bag and the lot is accepted or rejected basing on the oil content estimated from it. To avoid bias in testing, the manufacturer takes 3 samples from the each lot, one at the top, middle and bottom of the bag, mix the samples and test for the oil content.

The problem of interest is to estimate of the quality basing on the three samples and define a decision rule to accept or reject the lot. Such lots will be processed by means of SkSP-1. We will characterize this problem as SkSP-1 and study some issues relating to its performance.

SOME RESULTS ON SKSP-1

The principle of SkSP-1 is similar to that of CSP-1 except that one lot is considered as a unit. If (*i*, *f*) are the plan parameters and the probability of accepting a lot is P_a, then it can be shown that the percentage of lots accepted by SkSP is given by

$$L_{SK}(p) = \frac{(1-f)P_a^i + fP_a}{(1-f)P_a^i + f} \tag{5.1}$$

Since every lot is not inspected, some defective material will escape inspection and reach the customer. The average fraction of inspection is known to be

$$AFI_{SK} = \frac{f}{(1-f)P_a^i + f} \text{ and} \tag{5.2a}$$

$$ASN_{SK} = n^* \, AFI_{SK} \tag{5.2b}$$

The expression in (5.1) is considered as the OC of SkSP-1 and it depends on those parameters *i*, *f* and P_a. Suppose P_a = *p* known. Even then some fraction of defectives escape inspection. If $P_a = 0$ $L_{SK} = 0$ and if $P_a = 1$ $L_{SK} = 1$. Given the values of i and f the ability of SkSP to distinguish between good and bad lots depends on P_a.

Again for a given P_a we can find several combinations of i and f, which give the same protection against incorrect acceptance of lots under SkSP.

In the following section we discuss the case of a specific inspection procedure used to sentence the lots and examine its effect on SkSP.

THE ONE-THIRD SPLIT-LOT INSPECTION METHOD

This is a novel method in which a lot of fixed quantity and standard dimension is considered for acceptance or rejection. Lots should be identical with respect to size and quantity. They should be amenable for making the top, middle and bottom zones of equal size. The hypothesis is that the quality like moisture content, grain size,.etc is uniform with in the lot. A sample of fixed size using an instrument is drawn from each zone and the material is tested for quality.

Let 'Y' be the random variable denoting the quality characteristic in the lot. Define Y_j be the value of Y from the jth zone for j =1,2,3.

Assume that $Y \sim N(\mu,\sigma^2)$ and $Y_j \sim N(\mu_j,\sigma^2)$ for j = 1,2,3 with σ^2 known. An unbiased estimator of μ is given by

$$\hat{u} = \overline{y} = \frac{\sum_{j=1}^{3} y_j}{3} \tag{5.3}$$

$$\text{and } V(\overline{y}) = \sigma^2/3 \tag{5.4}$$

Let the decision rule to accept the lot be specified by the lower specification limit, LSL. Then the lot will be accepted if ≥ LSL. We can also use the weighted mean in place of and accept the lot if ≥ L. The weights w_j can be chosen so as to

$$\bar{y}_w = \frac{\sum_{j=1}^{3} w_j y_j}{\sum_{j=1}^{3} w_j} \tag{5.5}$$

reflect the quality level in j^{th} zone of the lot. If $w_j = 1$ for all j (5.5) reduces to (5.3). Thus in order to dispose a lot we are indirectly using a sampling plan with fixed size $n = 3$. The decision rule however depends on the acceptance factor 'k' which satisfies

$$\bar{y} \geq LSL + k\sigma \tag{5.6}$$

where k is called *acceptance factor*.

The probability of accepting a lot is then given by

$$\begin{aligned} P_a = L(\mu) &= P\{\bar{y} \geq LSL + k\sigma \mid \mu\} \\ &= P\left\{\frac{\bar{y}-\mu}{\sigma/\sqrt{3}} \geq \frac{LSL + k\sigma - \mu}{\sigma/3} \mid \mu\right\} \\ &= P\left\{Z \geq \left(\frac{LSL-\mu}{\sigma/\sqrt{3}}\right) + \sqrt{3}k \mid \mu\right\} \\ &= P\left\{Z \geq \sqrt{3}\left(\frac{LSl-\mu}{\sigma} + k\right) \mid \mu\right\} \end{aligned} \tag{5.7}$$

$$\Rightarrow \quad P_a = L(\mu) = 1 - \Phi\left\{\sqrt{3}\left(\frac{LSL-\mu}{\sigma} + k\right)\right\}$$

Thus P_a is a function of n, k and μ, where μ is the true mean of the incoming lots. The value of k is chosen such that $L(\text{AQL}) \geq 1-\alpha$.

$$\Rightarrow \Phi\left\{\sqrt{3}\left(\frac{LSL-\mu}{\sigma} + k\right)\right\} \geq 1-\alpha$$

$$\Rightarrow \sqrt{3}\left(\frac{LSL-\mu}{\sigma} + k\right) \geq Z_{1-\alpha}$$

$$\Rightarrow \left\{\frac{LSL-\mu}{\sigma}\right\}+k \geq \frac{Z_{1-\alpha}}{\sqrt{3}}$$

$$\Rightarrow k \geq \frac{Z_{1-\alpha}}{\sqrt{3}}-\left\{\frac{LSL-\mu}{\sigma}\right\}$$

If we write $Z_{LSL} = \frac{LSL-\mu}{\sigma}$, then the condition on k is $k \geq \frac{Z_{1-\alpha}}{\sqrt{3}} - Z_{LSL}$.

Taking k value at the equality, we get the *minimum acceptance factor* (Mittag & Rinne[28] (1993))

$$k^* = \frac{Z_{1-\alpha}}{\sqrt{3}} - Z_{LSL} \tag{5.8}$$

Thus the sampling plan will have $n = 3$ and $k = k^*$. Suppose $k^* = 2.0$ and $Z_{1-\alpha} = 1.645$.

Then the lot will be accepted, if $\sqrt{3}\left(Z_{ISL}+2.0\right) \geq 1.645$.

Let the LSL be 5.0 and the sample mean be $\overline{y} = 4.67$ with known $\sigma = 0.80$. Then $Z_{LSL} = 0.4125$ and the lot is accepted.

The value of P_a obtained by this method can be embedded in SkSP performance measures.

ESTIMATION OF μ & σ^2

The weighted mean from the three sample values is

$\overline{y}_w = \frac{\sum_{j=1}^{3} w_j y_j}{\sum_{j=1}^{3} w_j}$, where w_j is the weight given to the sample drawn from the jth position.

If we write $v_j = \dfrac{w_j}{\sum_{j=1}^{3} w_j}$ then $\bar{y}_w = v_1 y_1 + v_2 y_2 + v_3 y_3$ such that $v_1 + v_2 + v_3 = 1$.

The weights v_1, v_2 and v_3 can be chosen so as to reflect the quality gradient within lot supplied by a particular vendor. For instance, the vector [0.5 , 0.2, 0.3] indicates 50 per cent weightage for the material on the top of the lot, 20 per cent at middle and 30 per cent at bottom. This vector may change from vendor to vendor or from time to time for the same vendor.

Now $V(\bar{y}_w) = \sigma^2 \left(v_1^2 + v_2^2 + v_3^2\right)$. If σ^2 is not known, we can estimate it from the vendor's quality history by the following steps.

1. For each lot record y_1, y_2, y_3 from the three zones.
2. Calculate $\bar{y}_w = v_1 y_1 + v_2 y_2 + v_3 y_3$ for known values of v_1, v_2, v_3.
3. Calculate R_i = Max (y_1, y_2, y_3) – Min (y_1, y_2, y_3) for all $i = 1, 2, 3, ..m$. where m is the number of lots.
4. Calculate $\bar{\mu} = \bar{\bar{y}}_w = \dfrac{\sum_{i=1}^{m} \bar{y}_{wi}}{m}$.
5. An estimate of σ^2 is $\hat{\sigma}^2 = \dfrac{\bar{R}}{d_2}$, where $\bar{R} = \dfrac{\sum_{i=1}^{m} R_i}{m}$ = and d_2 is the scaling factor obtained from tables. For $n = 3$, $d_2 = 1.693$.

We can now calculate $k^* = \dfrac{Z_{1-\alpha}}{\sqrt{3}} - Z_{LSL}$ and find $L(\mu)$ using (5.7).

Using this $\hat{\sigma}^2, P_a$, P_a can be calculated with the procedure given in section 5.4. This P_a can be embedded in a predefined

SkSP-1 and the performance measures can be studied. Consider the following illustration:

Illustration 5.1

The quality characteristic in each lot at Top, Middle and Bottom are known to have Normal distribution with means $\mu_1 = 10.2$, $\mu_2 = 9.8$, $\mu_3 = 10.1$ and σ^2 is not known. It means $Y_1 \sim N(10.2, \sigma^2)$, $Y_2 \sim N(9.8, \sigma^2)$ and $Y_3 \sim N(10.1, \sigma^2)$. The available data from sample lots supplied by a vendor are given in table-5.1.

Table 5.1: Y_j values for different lots. $j = 1 \rightarrow$ Top, $j = 2 \rightarrow$ Middle, $j = 3 \rightarrow$ Bottom

Lot No	Top	Middle	Bottom
1	10.0	10.0	10.9
2	9.6	9.7	10.6
3	10.3	9.8	9.7
4	10.8	9.8	9.5
5	10.8	9.0	9.9
6	11.1	9.5	10.8
7	9.1	10.4	10.7
8	10.1	9.9	10.3
9	10.7	10.2	9.4
10	9.7	9.6	9.9
11	9.9	9.2	10.0
12	9.4	10.6	9.7
13	9.3	10.0	9.8
14	9.7	9.7	10.5
15	9.8	10.1	10.1
16	9.1	9.0	9.8
17	9.9	10.5	9.7
18	10.0	8.8	10.9
19	10.3	9.6	10.6
20	10.0	11.5	10.3

We wish to estimate the lot quality and its standard deviation. Suppose $v_1 = 0.5$, $v_2 = 0.2$ and $v_3 = 0.3$ are weights.

Then $\hat{\mu} = 10.0$ and $\hat{\sigma}^2 = \frac{\overline{R}}{d_2} = \frac{1.0}{1.693} = 1.6143 \Rightarrow \hat{\sigma} = 0.4831$.

Let the LSL be 8.0, so that $Z_{LSL} = -4.1509$. We get $k^* = 5.101$. Using (5.6) we accept the lot if $\overline{y}_w \geq 10.4643$ and reject otherwise.

Suppose for the incoming lot, the three sample measurements are 9.5, 10.8 and 13.5. The weighted mean becomes 11.0 (> 10.4643) and the decision is to *accept* the lot. If the sample values for another lot are 7.5, 12.0 and 10.8 $\overline{y}_w$ will be 9.4 (< 10.4643) and the lot will be *rejected.*

PERFORMANCE MEASURES OF THE PROCEDURE

Suppose the input parameters are LSL = 8, $\sigma = 0.4831$ and $k = 5.101$. Assume that the lots are processed by SkSP with $i = 4$

Table-5.2: Values of OC and ASN against mean

μ	L(p)	$L_{SK}(p)$	ASN_{SK}
9.0	0.0000	0.0000	3
9.2	0.0000	0.0000	3
9.4	0.0001	0.0001	3
9.6	0.0010	0.0010	3
9.8	0.0086	0.0086	3
10.0	0.0480	0.0480	3
10.2	0.1717	0.1745	3
10.4	0.4088	0.4682	3
10.6	0.6867	0.8341	2
10.8	0.8856	0.9669	1
11.0	0.9726	0.9940	1
11.2	0.9958	0.9992	1

and $f = 0.2$, by using the one-third split-lot as reference plan. Then for different values of the incoming quality μ (for the whole lot) the OC function $L(\mu)$ of the reference plan, the OC function $L_{SK}(\mu)$ of SkSP and its ASN function denoted by ASN_{SK} are shown in table-5.2.The behavior of OC function of SkSP and reference plan is exhibited in the following figure-5.1, figure-5.2 and figure-5.3 respectively.

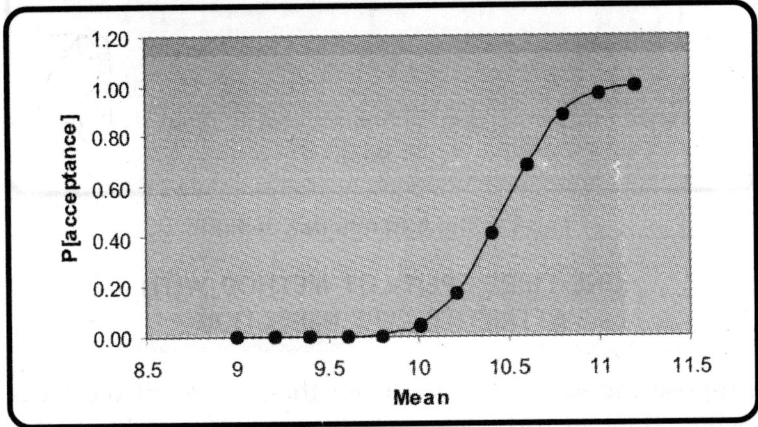

Fig. 5.1: The OC function of split-lot sampling plan

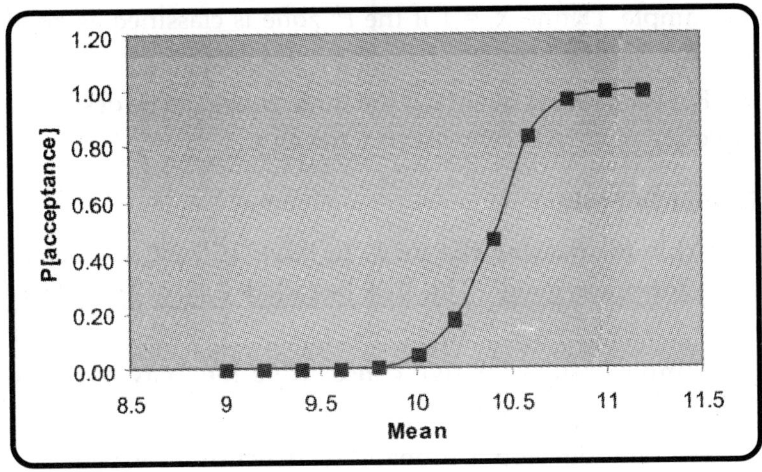

Fig. 5.2: Percentage of lots accepted by SkSP

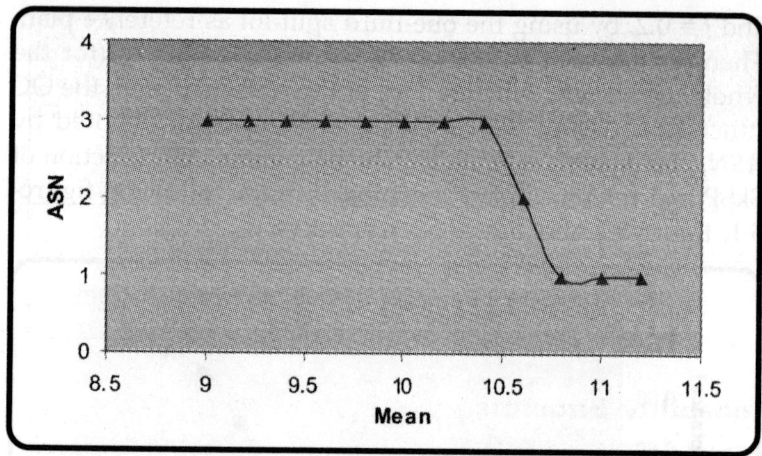

Fig. 5.3: The ASN function of SkSP

ONE-THIRD SPLIT-LOT METHOD WITH ATTRIBUTE TYPE NSPECTION

Suppose the sample drawn from the jth zone of the lot is inspected by an attribute type judgement. The quality in this zone will be classified as good or poor basing on the result of the sample. Define $X_j = 1$ if the ith zone is classified as good and $X_j = 0$ otherwise.

For each lot the quality at the three zones can be described tuple (x_1, x_2, x_3) where $x_j = 1$ or 0 for all j.

Decision Rule

One rule for passing the lot is to have at least two out of three zones are 'good'.. This may be called '*2 out of 3 acceptance rule*'.

Sample results for five consecutive lots may have the following quality grades.

We now develop a probability structure to explain the decision rule.

Lot	Zone			Decision
	Top	Middle	Bottom	
1	1	1	0	Accept
2	0	1	1	Accept
3	1	0	0	Reject
4	1	1	1	Accept
5	0	0	1	Reject

Probability Structure

Define p_j = P[j^{th} zone is good] and 1-p_j = P[j^{th} zone is poor]. These probabilities can be estimated from the quality history of the vendor. There are only four mutually exclusive cases that would recommend the acceptance of the lot.

Assuming independence of successive lots, these events are given below along with their occurrence probabilities

Vector (event)	Probability
[1 1 0]	$p_1p_2(1-p_3)$
[1 0 1]	$p_1(1-p_2)p_3$
[0 1 1]	$(1-p_1)p_2p_3$
[1 1 1]	$p_1p_2p_3$

Hence $P_a = p_1p_2(1-p_3) + p_1(1-p_2)p_3 + (1-p_1)p_2p_3 + p_1p_2p_3$. (5.9)

Suppose $p_j = p$ for all j. It means the probability of being good is the same at top, middle and bottom of the lot.

Then P_a becomes $p^2(1-p)+ p^2(1-p)+ p^2(1-p)+p^3$

$\Rightarrow 3\,p^2(1-p)+p^3$

$\Rightarrow 3p^2-2p^3$ (5.10)

Given the vector of probabilities $[p_1 p_2 p_3]$ we can determine P_a for each lot and adopt this in the SkSP.

OC OF SkSP-1 WITH SPLIT-LOT INSPECTION BY VARIABLES

Substituting (5.10) in (5.1) with known i and f, the OC function with equal probabilities can be stated in open form as

$$L_{Sk}(p) = \frac{(1-f)\left(3p^2-2p^3\right)^i + f\left(3p^2-2p^3\right)}{(1-f)\left(3p^2-2p^3\right)^i + f} \qquad (5.11)$$

Suppose $p_1 = 0.9$, $p_2 = 0.7$ and $p_3 = 0.8$ for given batch of lots supplied by a vendor. From (5.9) we get $P_a = 0.902$. It means for this vendor the acceptance probability of single lot (bag) is 0.902. Over a period of time these probabilities may undergo transition for the same vendor, in which case the acceptance probability will change.

If SkSP is adopted with given i and f, one can estimate the OC value using this P_a. If each zone within the lot has equal probability p of being good then the lot will be accepted with probability $(3p^2\text{-}2p^3)$. The corresponding OC of SkSP will have an open form given in (5.11).

Observations

In this chapter a novel method of sampling inspection is explored to estimate the quality in the lot. Procedures are developed for both variable and attribute type inspection. The salient aspect of this study is that the one-third split-lot inspection method acts as a *reference plan*, which SkSP-1 usually does not specify.

6

Conclusion and Scope for Further Research

The following conclusions can be drawn from the work reported in this thesis.

1. Designing of a sampling plan can be done effectively with the help of Excel worksheet functions instead of referring to sampling tables.
2. Standard algorithms like Guenther's algorithm, Graf *et al* one-step method and the Peach-Littauer's algorithm can be effectively implemented. Guenther's algorithm however requires a special tool called Circular Reference along with solver, which are available in Excel.
3. A new search procedure called Modified Graf *et al* Method (MGM) is developed which is based on Graf *et al* formulae and the Solver option in Excel. The

method ultimately gives a quick solution to (n,c) of Single Sampling Plan. It is shown that the plan provided by MGM agrees with the one developed by Guenther's algorithm.

4. The optimal values of the SkSP parameters are derived in Excel by using reference plan obtained from MGM. It is shown that the OC, ASN and the AOQL of SkSP depend on the reference plan and the MGM based reference plan performs well. The AOQL also increases when the RQL is increased for the given reference plan.
5. Inspection errors are characterized by using Beta distribution of type-1 with equal parameters. The apparent fraction defective and its expectation are developed.
6. Error adjusted plans are developed for Single Sampling by using Beta(m,m) distribution for Type-1 and Type-2 errors. The effect of Error Mean-Adjusted plan on SkSP is also studied. It is observed that as m increases the OC curve of SkSP becomes steeper while the ASN increases rapidly.
7. A novel but practical method of inspection in which one sample is taken from top, middle and bottom of each lot (bag) is explored and a method of estimating the quality of the material by variable type of inspection is developed. Procedure is also developed for attribute type of inspection also. By taking such a practice as reference plan, an inspection procedure of type SkSP-1 is developed.

SCOPE FOR FURTHER RESEARCH

Here are some possible extensions that can be studied from the results of this thesis.

- The spreadsheet solutions can be extended to other type of plans.

- Inspection errors can be characterized by other distributions in the range [0,1].
- The effect of Beta distribution in this thesis is limited to each type of error separately. It is more interesting to consider a bivariate Beta distribution with possible truncation. This would have theoretical importance.
- The one-third split-lot method developed in chapter-5 can be further studied in a Bayesian set up with prior distribution observed from the vendor's quality history.

Bibliography

1. Abraham.F.L(1971), "A Graphical Method of Parameter Selection for CSP-1, CSP-2, and CSP-R Under a Non-replacement Assumption", *Journal of Quality Technology*, Vol. 3, No. 1,2-5.
2. Anderson, M.T. and Greenberg, B.S. and Stokes, S.L (2001), "Acceptance Sampling with Rectification when Inspection Errors are Present", *Journal of Quality Technology,* Vol. 33, No. 4, pp. 493-505.
3. Beainy.I and Case K.E (1981), "A Wide Variety of AOQ and ATI Performance Measures with and without Inspection Error", *Journal of Quality Technology*, Vol. 13, No. 1, 1-9.
4. Brush.G and Hoadley.B (1990), "Estimating Outgoing Quality Using the Quality Measurement Plan", *Technometrics*, Feb. 1990, Vol. 32, No.1, 31-41.
5. Chakraborthy.S and Umesh Kumar, R. (1989), "Analysis of Inspection Error Through GERT", *Sankya,* Vol. 51, Series. B, Pt. 1, pp.125-133.
6. Chun.Y.H and Rinks.D.B (1998), "Three Types of Producer's and Consumer's Risks in the Single Sampling Plan", *Journal of Quality Technology*, Vol. 30, No. 3, 254-268.
7. Craig.C (1981), "A Note on the Construction of Double Sampling Plans", *Journal of Quality Technology*, Vol. 13, No. 3, 192-200.
8. Dodge, H.F. (1943) A Sampling Plan for Continuous Production, *Annals of Mathematical Statistics* 14, 264-269.
9. Dodge, H.F. (1955b) Skip-lot Sampling Plan. *Industrial Quality Control* 11, 3-5.

10. Dodge, H.F. and Perry, R.L. (1971), "A System of Skip-lot Plans for Lot by Lot Inspection, American Society for Quality Control", *Technometrics,* 469-477.

11. Ghosh, D.T.(1988), "The Continuous Sampling Plan that Minimizes the Amount of Inspection", *Sankya*, Vol. 50,Series-B, pt. 3, pp. 412-427.

12. Ghosh, D.T. (1989), On the Near Optimum Continuous Sampling Plan CSP-2 (with $k = i$) to Minimize the Amount of Inspection and Its Performance as Compared to Optimum CSP-1 Plan, *Sankya*, 51, 390-415.

13. Ghosh, D.T. (1990) The Optimum Continuous Sampling Plan CSP-2($k=i$) that Minimizes the Amount of Inspection, *Opsearch*, Vol. 27, No.1, pp. 31-38.

14. Graf, U., Henning, H.J., Stange, K., Wilrich, P.Th., (1987), Formeln und Tabellen der angewandten mathematischen Statistik, *3rd ed., Springer Verlag,Berlin/Heidelberg.*

15. Greenberg, B.S. and Stokes, S.L (1992), "Estimating Non-conformance Rates after Zero Defect Sampling with Rectification", *Technometrics* 34, pp. 203-213.

16. Greenberg,.B.S. and Stokes, S.L (1995), "Repetitive Testing in the Presence of Inspection Errors", *Technometrics* 37, pp. 102-111.

17. Guenther, W.C (1969), Use of Binomial, Hyper Geometric and Poisson Tables to Obtain Sampling Plans, *Journal of Quality Technology,* 1, 105-109.

18. Hahn.G.J. (1974), "Minimum Size Sampling Plans", *Journal of Quality Technology*, Vol. 6, No. 3, 121-127.

19. Hahn.G.J. (1986), "Estimating the Per Cent Non-conforming in the Accepted Product After Zero Defect Sampling", *Journal of Quality Technology*, Vol. 18, No. 3, pp. 182-188.

20. Hailey, W.A. (1980), Minimum Sample Size Single Sampling Plans: A Computerized Approach. *Journal of Quality Technology* 12, 230-235.

21. Harichandra, K and Srivenkataramana.T(1982), "Link Sampling for Attributes", *Communications in Statistics—Theory and Methods* 11, pp. 1855-1868.

22. Johnson, N.L., Kotz.S, and Rodriguez, R.N. (1986), "Statistical Effects of Imperfect Inspection Sampling: II. Double Sampling and Link Sampling", *Journal of Quality Technology*, Vol. 18, No. 2,116-138.

23. Lieberman.G.J.(1953), "A Note on Dodge's Continuous Sampling Plans", *Annals of Mathematical Statistics*, 24, 480- 484.

24. Lieberman.G.J and Resnikoff.G.J (1955), "Sampling Plans for inspection by Variables", *Journal of American Statistical Association*, 50, 457-517

25. Lieberman, G.J and Solomon, H (1953), "Multilevel Continuous Sampling Plans", *Annals of Mathematical Stitistics*,26,686-704.

26. Lindsay, B.G (1985), "Errors in Inspection: Integer Parameter Maximum Likelihood in a Finite Population", *Journal of American Statistical Association*, 879-885.

27. Martz.H.F and Zimmer.W.J (1990), "A Non-parametric Bayes Empirical Bayes Procedure for Estimating the Per cent Non-conforming in Accepted Lots", *Journal of Quality Technology*, Vol. 22, No. 2, 95-104.

28. Mittag, H.J. and Rinne, H (1993), Statistical Methods of Quality Assurance, Chapman & Hall.

29. Mood.M (1943), "On the Dependence of Sampling Inspection Plans upon Population Distribution", *Annals of Mathematical Statistics,* 415-425.

30. Peach, P. and Littauer, S.B (1946), A Note on Sampling Inspection, *Annals of Mathematical Statistics, 17, 81-84*

31. Perry, R.L. (1973a), Skip-lot Sampling Plans *Journal of Quality Technology* 5,123-130.

32. Perry, R.L. (1973b), Two-level Skip Lot Sampling Plans Operating Characteristic Properties. *Journal of Quality Technology* 5, 160-166.

33. Sampath Kumar, V.S.(1984), A Tightened m-level Continuous Sampling Plan for Morkov Dependent Production Process, IIE Transactions, Vol. 16, 3rd November.

34. Sarma K.V.S. (2002), Statistics Made Simple—Do It Yourself on PC, Prentice Hall India.

35. Schilling, E.G. (1982), Acceptance Sampling in Quality Control, *Marcel Dekker*, New York/Basel.

36. Snyder.D.C and Storer.R.F (1972), "Single Sampling Plans Given an AQL, LTPD, Producer and Consumer Risks" *Journal of Quality Technology*, Vol. 4, No. 3, 168-171.

37. Soundararajan, V.(1975), "Maximum Allowable Per cent Defective (MAPD): Single Sampling Inspection by Attributes Plan", *Journal of Quality Technology*, Vol. 7, No. 4, 173-177

38. Soundararajan, V. and Vijayaraghavan, R. (1989), A New System of Skip-lot Sampling Inspection Plans of Type SkSP-3, Quality for Progress and Development, Proceedings of the Papers Presented at the First Asian Congress on Quality and Reliability, Delhi, November, 1989.

39. Suresh, K.K., Radhakrishnan, R and Alamelu, R (2002) "Matching of Continuous Sampling", Proceedings of the National Symposium on Statistical Methods and Applications Organized by Annamalai University, 127-137.

40. Suresh, K.K., Radhakrishnan, R and Kavitha, M.T. (2002) "Construction and Comparison of TNT- (n_1, n_2/O)" *Proceedings of the National Symposium on Statistical Methods and Applications Organized by Annamalai University*, 138-144.

41. Wadsworth, H.M. and Stephens, K.S. and Gidfrey, E.B. (1986), Quality Control , *Wiley*, New York.

42. Zalavsky, A. (1988), "Estimating Non-conformity Rates in c-Defect Sampling". *Journal of Quality Technology*, Vol. 20, No. 4, pp. 248-258.

Index